Sweat & Blood

THE DIARY OF A CIVIL WAR SOLDIER

Stephen H. Baldwin, circa 1880

Stephen Hamlin Baldwin
Civil War Veteran

By
DAVID BEN FOSTER
Great-Great-Grandson

Copyright© 2015 David Ben Foster

ISBN: 978-0-9893583-6-1
Library of Congress Control Number: 2014933633

All rights reserved. Except for use in any review, the reproduction or utilization of this work in whole or in part in any form by any electronic, mechanical or other means, now known or hereafter invented, including xerography, photocopying and recording, or in any information storage or retrieval system, is forbidden without the written permission of the author.

Sweat and Blood – The Diary of a Civil War Soldier is a biographical work of non-fiction.

Published by Blossom Book Publishing
Medina, Ohio

Printed in the United States of America

FOREWORD

During the decades after the Civil War Stephen H. Baldwin was known to preach wearing a visual aid of his own construction, a wooden chain carved from a thirteen-foot log, complete with lock and key. Baldwin was chained in another way. His role in the war to make men free had forever bound him to chronic disease and emotional turmoil that would only much later be called post-traumatic stress disorder.

When he enlisted in 1862 Baldwin seemed a template for a Union war hero; the sharpshooting son of Ohio abolitionists, descended from Revolutionary stock, who left his young bride to come to the aid of Father Abraham. His war was defined by the rivers of America's muscular midsection. The Ohio, Mississippi, Yazoo and then the Arkansas carried him to Fort Hindman, a Confederate bastion that his regiment, the 96th Ohio Infantry helped capture in early 1863. A few months later he received a medical discharge and returned home.

Treatises about the Civil War seldom chronicle the fate of the fighting men that it traumatized. Perhaps their postwar disorders somehow made them less accessible or less creditable to those who shaped the flow of our remembrance of that epic struggle. Baldwin's story has been retrieved by author and great-great-grandson David Ben Foster. In his recent volume, Sweat & Blood, based on the diary and letters of his ancestor, Foster has forged new shackles; Baldwin is now chained to our memory of the Civil War. That the author is a five generations removed from the title character is a misnomer. This well written, profusely interested tale raises him to first place among the Baldwin clan.

Tim Beatty
Assistant Curator of Manuscripts at the
Western Reserve Historical Society

DEDICATION

I would like to dedicate this book to my sister Sandra Davis for her unselfish love and dedication to others. She shares my love and passion for our rich family heritage which has created an even stronger bond between us. Many of the photos found in this book were supplied by her.

ACKNOWLEDGEMENTS

I would like to thank my fellow compatriots, Dick Fetzer and Timothy Ward of the Western Reserve Society Sons of the American Revolution for their encouragement in fostering my involvement in the many lineage organizations that I am a member of today. I have come to appreciate my lineage even more deeply since becoming involved.

A special thanks to Barbara Griffith of the Cuyahoga Portage Chapter of the Daughters of the American Revolution for supplying me with the Camp Dennison cut-outs of the restored buildings by the DAR.

I would also like to thank my sister, Nancy Foster Fisher, for her contribution of our ancestor's photos.

PREFACE

In 1638, the *Martin* arrived in New England with three brothers and their widowed mother. Their father, Sylvester Baldwin, died on June 21st almost a month before their arrival. The sons, Richard, John, and Joseph eventually moved to Connecticut, and from their descendants came statesmen serving in the Congress of the United States, and one had become Speaker of the House; several became physicians, attorneys, industrialists, philanthropists, ministers, and many more professional occupations. Descendants, John Baldwin (1799-1884), had been a co-founder of Baldwin Wallace College in Berea, Ohio, and in 1862, Dwight Hamilton Baldwin (1821-1899), a reed organ and violin teacher, opened his music store in Cincinnati, Ohio, and later created and designed the Baldwin Piano.

It was during John and Dwight's life that a contemporary nephew had been born, Stephen Hamlin Baldwin (1836-1923). He is my great-great-grandfather, a Civil War veteran, and the reason that I've written this book.

This biographical work about Stephen has been written in his own words as found in his well-kept diaries that he had written during and after the Civil War.

I have also used information gleaned from his family Bible and letters he had received. Within this book you will find photos that are rich in history and help tell the story of this lonely soldier who truly invested his sweat and blood in fighting for that which he believed in.

Stephen had been a farmer, a hunter, a crack-shot marksman, a soldier, an entrepreneur, a skilled craftsman in wood, crystal, and marble, and a minister.

I look upon these treasured remnants of this American Patriot, which are now in my possession, with awe as I realize the disparaging conditions of which the American heroes of this monumental war endured. My great, great grandfather, like most soldiers of that time, suffered tremendous physical and psychological consequences which led to the difficulties he had to endure once the war had ended. And yet, from his faithful service and sacrifice, he left behind a legacy of patriotism that I am proud of and speak of every chance I get.

In the summer of 1862, after reading the newspaper's *"cry for volunteers... in every village and town,"* Stephen and his father, Roswell, decided that he should do what was "in his heart." Even though he had just recently married his wife, Eleanor Miller on January 17, 1862, at the age of 26, Stephen joined the Union Army August 11, 1862. He did so *"with a trembling hand... to be a mark for men to shoot at,"* he later wrote in his diary years after the war.

He left in September and boarded a train to Covington, Kentucky. His letters were optimistic speaking of the brevity of the war, his new duties, and because he was older than most of the soldiers in his regiment, he felt that *"the boys had enough to think about,"* so he was more responsible and wanted to care for the younger men in some way. Many older soldiers had this sense of watchfulness.

During the war he had traveled in Ohio, Indiana, Kentucky, Tennessee, and down the Mississippi River to Louisiana and back up the Mississippi River to Fort Arkansas. After being in the war for almost a year he spoke of witnessing carnage and death that he had not seen during the killing in previous months along the Yazoo River. Over the course of his eighteen months in the war, fifteen of which were on the battlefield, he had been hospitalized three times and during all of these hospitalizations he longed to go home. One doctor told him that he was suffering from "a soldier's heart," which he understood to mean that there was something wrong with his heart. When in fact the doctor was referring to what is known today as post-traumatic stress disorder (PTSD.)

Because of the horrific conditions of the war, life was exceptionally difficult for Stephen after he returned home. He suffered from debilitating bouts of despair and terrifying memories that almost paralyzed him by making daily activities nearly impossible. He indeed had what was then called a "soldier's heart".

Studies by several organizations such as medical and psychiatric associations have completed studies from more than 30,000 medical records of Union soldiers showing that 20 % developed persistent mental and physical disease. Many factors were figured in the reports such as the percentage of company killed, age when enlisted, witnessing death, handling dead bodies, and being a prisoner of war (which increased the percentages).

Dr. Roxane Cohen Silver PhD, from the University of California, sent an Abstract study done by her and two other associates in 2006, and in it that study, they claim to have taken 17,700 medical records out of a sample of 35,730 records, which revealed that a veteran having signs of cardiovascular, GI, or nervous disease were previously classified as having one or more or more ailments. Gastrointestinal ailments included chronic diarrhea and related GI conditions. Nervous disease included paranoia, psychosis, hallucinations, illusions, insomnia, confusion, hysteria, sensory problems, delusions, and violent behavior. Here is an excerpt from the report:

> One objective measure of intimate violence, percentage of company killed, predicted a 51% increase incidence of unique disease ailments. Percentage of company killed is likely a powerful variable because it serves as a proxy for various traumatic stressors, such as witnessing death or dismemberment, handling dead bodies, traumatic loss of comrades, realizing one's own imminent death, killing others, and being helpless to prevent others' deaths... Not only was the Civil War the beginning of a recognition of mental health problems caused by war, labeled "irritable heart syndrome," many recognize the Civil War as laying the roots of modern cardiology.

Especially following the Battle of Arkansas Post, Stephen had developed most of the classical symptoms associated with PTSD. He suffered with feeling the horror of the past through flashbacks that would occur suddenly after such things as hearing a gun fired from a hunter, or witnessing a tragic accident, or the loss of loved ones. His condition was especially heightened when four of his children died over a span of twelve years. He went out of his way to avoid confrontations that would set off painful memories. Since soldiers often used their own weapons in the war, Stephen had used his hunting revolver from when he was a young man. Oddly, he quit using his revolver two months before his discharge, selling it to his brother-in-law after they had left Arkansas Post.

Even though he had wanted out of the war so badly, it's peculiar that he started collecting war memorabilia a few years after his discharge. Prior to joining the army, Stephen had a passion and enjoyment for hunting, and was considered quite the marksman. However, all that changed after the war and in his diary he never again mentions hunting as a joy. He only hunted one time after the war out of pure necessity for food.

Difficulty followed him incessantly as the years passed. The inability to express his feelings to his family, employment conflicts, despair, and anxiety issues such as crying spells with unexplained shaking so bad that he was inconsolable.

At the age of 56, Stephen entered the ministry but was never assigned a church because of his PTSD, chronic diarrhea, and other illnesses which made him unfit for the pastorate. His temperament was seldom warm, and he could be viewed as cold which was also unbecoming as a minister. He found solace in writing poetry, hymns, and religious articles for newspapers.

He never lost his pride for the Baldwin name, or his mother's surname, Hamlin.

He prided himself in the memories of Baldwin stories spoken at reunions, or around his father's table. The Joseph Baldwin family had come to New England in 1638, and throughout his upbringing, Stephen heard the stories of the adventures, the inventions, entrepreneurs, abolitionists, and soldiers who had given their sweat and blood for America as well.

The 13-foot chain was hand carved by Stephen Baldwin from a single log. It has continuous interlocking links that represent each book of the Bible. Thirty-nine links are stained in mahogany to represent the Old Testament and twenty-seven links are stained in gold to represent the New Testament. It also has a carved key at one end and a carved lock at the other end. This chain was used in his ministry when he was illustrating the importance of the connection between both Testaments of the Bible.

DAVID BEN FOSTER

A UNIQUE CHAIN

Used In Bible Lecture By Former Mottown Minister.

Rev. Stephen H. Baldwin of Morrow county was in Alliance Monday visiting old friends. Mr. Baldwin formerly preached at Mottown but now lectures and teaches the Bible in his own original way. One device in illustration he uses is a huge chain thirteen feet long and made of one piece of Norway pine. There is a link for every book of the Bible, the 39 representing the books of the old Testament, the wood being oiled and left in its natural color. The 27 links representing the books of the new Testament are decorated with gold. A swivel, representing the interim between the time of Malachi and the coming of Christ, joins the two sets of links. The whole is used by Mr. Baldwin to illustrate the truth of the Bible and the teachings of Christ.

A newspaper article appeared in a Newark, Ohio publication. The article talks about the Reverend, Stephen Baldwin and his hand carved chain representing the Bible.

Stephen carved many items from crystal but his most cherished piece was this small crystal Bible which measures 1 ¼" x 2".

CONTENTS

The Early Years	1
Eleanor Miller and Enlistment in the Union Army	8
The War Experiences	16
Returning Home	45
Farming and Other Businesses	48
Call to the Ministry	56
Post Traumatic Stress Disorder of Stephen Hamlin Baldwin	69
References	71
Appendix	72

THE EARLY YEARS

TAKEN FROM STEPHEN BALDWIN'S DIARIES:

"I was born in the year of our Lord 1836 on the 14th of November, the day on which President Van Buren was elected. I was born to Roswell and Martha (Hamlin) Baldwin in Stark County, Ohio about fourteen miles from the county seat in a small village called Harrisburg. My father was a farmer and a mechanic who owned a small farm of seventy-five acres through which there ran a beautiful stream called Beech Creek that flows from Berlin Lake. There were an abundance of fish especially Black Sucker and sunfish. There was an abundance of timber nearby: Poplar, Walnut, Chestnut, and Oak, so my father built a sawmill.

"In 1837 my brother Walter was born. My father farmed and put the mill in operation. Years passed of my boyhood days. I played at the mill and found much pleasure, as I would sport around the creek with its crystal ripples passing over the numerous limestone and pebbles. Here I learned to swim, thanks to Joseph, my older brother. At first I mostly swam like a duck, but these days were happy days of enjoyment for boyish pleasure."

Stephen's father, Roswell, had moved from Atwater in Portage County, where he had been reared by his father, David Baldwin Jr., who had fought in the War of 1812 and then became a Justice of the Peace. Roswell moved to Stark County sometime after his first wife, Martha Gaskell, died in about 1827, leaving five children. In 1829, he married his second wife, Stephen's mother, Martha Hamlin, who had been born in Virginia.

The Baldwin's came to Atwater in 1802 from Wallingford, New Haven, Connecticut after the Revolutionary War. Stephen's great grandfather, David Baldwin Sr. had fought in the Revolutionary War. David Baldwin Sr. married Parnell Clark and they had ten children. One of those children was Stephen's great aunt who he had enjoyed hearing stories about. She had moved to Atwater in 1812 with her husband, Theophilus Anthony. Stephen had saved a picture of her in his boxes of memorabilia which is the only picture of any of the Baldwin Revolutionary War patriots and their families that had survived. The picture of Abigail Baldwin Anthony had been taken in c. 1830 when she was in Atwater. She was born on March 3, 1780, and married in 1800.

Abigail Baldwin Anthony, c. 1850s

"It had been a memorable time growing up along Beech Creek, but 'time changes the pursuits and pleasures of most of us, and misfortune comes unaware.'

My father was a good man and a good neighbor, but not so good to himself, for he would have to go into security, sometimes for other farmers, and then had to pay the debt himself at ten percent, which he did too often. What made things worse, my father took the Typhoid fever and suffered for ten weeks. My little baby brother, Walter, died from the fever."

After Roswell recovered from Typhoid, he sold the farm and mill at a considerable sacrifice, but was free of the security and other debt. While he was closing the farm sale, he contacted relatives in Logan County to find out if farm land was available and for what price. Family and neighbors all helped him pack and sort things according to what he would be able to take and what he would have to leave behind. The loaded wagon had been packed full, as they moved in the late spring of 1846.

"We moved to Logan County where we had relatives and friends, and one who especially helped us was my uncle Jerub Baldwin. We soon rented land to farm, but it was new and had many stumps, but now we were used to hard times. Our diet was mostly milk, bread, and mush. My father ran the new mill he had built, and my mother worked the loom.

"My father rented this small farm with a stream on it which brought me a bit of joy, and soon, I began to hunt woodchucks and got five cents per pelt. It was not long after that I had become quite a good hunter, killing dear, wolves, duck, and a bear from time to time. By the time I was twelve, I became a crack shot. This was my life until I was about 18, in the year 1854, when my parents and brother Joseph, all had a serious infection of some sort on their hands and couldn't work. My sister, Bertha, had married and moved away, and my little sister, Almyra, was too young to do anything, and the chores, which included getting wood, was on me, and I had a cold time of it.

"In the midst of all this, my father got word that the rent payment was due on the farm and soon found out that his attorney ran off to Utah with the money we gave him for the bank. He was now out of our reach, for he moved to a Mormon village.

"Hardship and hunger seemed to stare us in the face again. During these meddlesome trials, I realized how good my father was, for in all the hardships, he never used drink, and he was always honest.

"Of course, we had some advantage and that was the age of us boys, for we could do about a man's work, and as our land was further north, there was wild land in large tracts with an abundance of squirrels, pheasants, and turkeys. I was quite a hunter now, and I got the greatest of wild meat to live on. Again at this time, I almost made it a business. There was plenty of game.

In 1855 in Ohio, wild game was still quite prevalent. Deer could be hunted by day or by torch light at night near rivers and lakes. Turkeys were easy marks, and they were numerous. The real danger for a hunter, even if there were two or three hunters in a camp, was the wolf pack. Depending on how hungry they were, they were a carnivorous threat to man, horses, and farm animals.

"Once in a time, when I was out in the woods alone after night fell, to my surprise, my dog, Pink, came to me with his hair turned up and barking as if nearly to death. I stooped to listen and to see if I could spot eyes glaring at me from some monster wolf, but could not. I heard something trotting in the leaves, and when I moved towards it with my torch, it made a spring for it, and off it went with my dog chasing it, barking every jump. I did not want Pink to catch it, for a wolf that size can take down a man. The next day we heard of people who had seen a large wolf in the area. There were wolves north of us, and once in a while one would be seen passing through the woods where we lived.

I would often hunt several miles north of our farm, but as I grew older, my mind seemed dissatisfied with small game, for there were plenty of larger game animals like deer, wolves, and once in a while a bear.

"In about 1855, I went north of the county and became a better hunter. Naturally, after I had done some chores on the farm, I went hunting, which brought me great joy, and my pelts and food from hunting provided us with what we needed.

"Later, I got the fever for the wild in the northern counties, and asked three boys to go with me. We packed our guns, ammunition, and supplies into our wagon, and then we hooked up a team to pull our wagon with our goods and luggage. After almost a full day, we had found a suitable place and decided to fix camp. It was kind of an open place where we had made camp, and I was soon with gun on my shoulder and a revolver in pocket with bullets in my other pocket, and made for the woods. I was not long out till I got sight of a deer. It was alone crawling along under some willow, but it did not go far, for the steady aim I had on her, and the sure fire of the piece made it almost certainly my game. I pulled the trigger, and the loud report of my gun sent the news back to the camp that something had been killed. Two of the boys came running over to me, and we carried a fine young deer to our camp.

"During the night the wolves hauled around us, so we could not sleep, and our horses snorted and pawed the ground most of the night. Finally, at just about day light, we were able to sleep a bit. Later in the afternoon, one of those ugly fellows followed me for a mile, hoping to keep near me till after dark. This is when they rally their forces as they did sometimes to overpower their game, but I had no intention of being his prey. I did see some game, but couldn't get off a shot. I guess the wolf was on my mind. Most of the days, we had not seen a wolf, so hunting became profitable and pleasurable to do.

"We stayed in camp for a few more days until the boys got tired and wanted to go home. We took some time shooting at a mark, and then we put the team to the wagon, and put our game in the wagon and started for home. I had killed two deer, six possums, and several pheasants. Two of the other boys each killed a deer to take home. We had some laugh at Stanley, the young man we had expected to be the champion hunter, but he did not get any kind of game. He had made his brags that he would kill more than all of us put together. Just before we started out for home, he shot at a tomtit, and the little bird flew away crying, "Chickadee, chickadee." We mocked Stanley repeatedly saying, 'they call him the king of tomtit: chickadee, chickadee."

"We arrived home in due time, and our friends were glad to see us and glad to hear that we had a good trip. We had a good amount of game for only eleven days of hunting. Soon the season would pass, and farm chores or millwork would pick up.

"Something more important happened. My poor broken down parents needed some help, for they were in debt again, so I left my older brother Joseph, to stay with them, and I went some forty miles from home to work by the month. In that particular town, I had found that home was not everywhere that I took off my hat. I did not stay there long on account of the room and board, for the work hands ate the roughest food, while the family and visitors had plenty, and that roused my blood to such a pitch that I raised a ruckus with the man, and left him. I had no trouble most of the time getting work at a good price by the day or by the job. Other men had some difficulty finding this kind of work, but I had no trouble. I made more money working by the job. I worked as I pleased and could be my own boss. In this way, I managed to make about one hundred dollars a year for my parents, and pay for my clothes.

"While working away from my parent's control, I first learned to handle the cards, and for a month or so, I learned to play two or three games pretty well. Memory, what a jewel to have while thus engaged, brought thoughts of Father's fireside, the dear family altar, and mother around whom had been the old trumpet vine of affection, and all twined to making home what it was to us. Memory of Mother's love, advice, and the tenderness can never be erased by time. Father, the giant oak, the king of the forest could only represent the straightness of a man and his endurance. Memories of these things were too much for me to meet with a deck of cards in my pocked, the pocket the hands of Mother shaped and stitched for my benefit. Those memories prompted me to remove these emblems of Satan and destroy them. This was a grand victory and a turning point towards a better life. I labored another year after that summer to pay the home debt.

"I have not said everything about my schooling, for I did not get much of that until I turned twenty-one years old. I had studied around the old log fireplace *or by the dim flickering of a tallow candle. After I was twenty-one, I paid my tuition in our district and boarded at home. The next winter I went to school in Bellefontaine and attended the Union School and boarded with my uncle. I made every moment count that last term and advanced well, but it hadn't been long before I turned my attention to other matters.*

ELEANOR ("ELLEN") MILLER AND ENLISTMENT IN THE UNION ARMY

Stephen's sister Almyra Baldwin
circa 1870

Stephen's sister Lydia
circa 1870

"In the fall of 1860, I remember well when I was going home from work, about three and a half miles from home. I had seen two girls coming towards me. I did not know them at first, but I soon saw that one of them was my youngest sister Almyra. As they came up to me, they were both laughing, and my sister told me what they had been laughing about. She said to her friend, 'Here comes my man.' The other girl said, 'No, that is my man.' Then my sister gave me an introduction to the girl, Eleanor Miller that I thought to be very handsome. You may well suppose, I sought her favor, enjoyed her company, and after eighteen months we were married. Her parents were poor, yet respectable, but they had raised a lady who I loved."

Joseph Baldwin and his children. Circa 1895

Stephen and Eleanor Baldwin, circa 1882

"During this time, my brother Joseph had married and settled down on Father's place. That is when I had seriously thought of marriage, and the old saying was, 'there is a time for a man to paddle his own canoe.' I was almost twenty-six and had no money because I had to help Father with what I could spare. The same girl, Eleanor Miller, that I had met with my sister, I married on January 17, 1862. We were poor, but we were happy and enjoying life as well as people could in our circumstances. She was my morning star that arose and captured my view. We were both happy, and although we went to different churches, we were both Christian. She eventually went with me to the Methodist Church.

"Time never stops to wait. After about seven months, the cry of war was heard and the shout for volunteers was in every village and town in the land, for even the sound of musket and the boom of canon were heard, and the rebels had taken Fort Sumter. Seventy-five thousand soldiers were called out, and the rumor was that all our young men would have to go. Then in the summer of 1862, there was a call from President Lincoln for 300,000 Union soldiers, and we began to think there was no other way but to go and help fight the Southern rebels who were very hostile against us.

"After duly considering the chances of the draft, as we had expected that there would be, I thought it best to enlist. I had spoken to my parents and wife, who left the decision to me. Joseph said that he was proud of me. My father told me that he felt that I had made the proper decision. Mother and my wife were not as sure. When the time came on 11th day of August 1862, I signed the roll with a trembling hand. Although my heart was in my throat because of leaving my young wife and aged parents who were suffering almost to death at the thought of me going to be a mark for some men to shoot at. Harper's Weekly all across the north, brought the plea from President Lincoln for volunteers. My father, with the newspaper in his hand, reminded me of my great grandfather, David Baldwin, who had fought in the Revolutionary War, and my grandfather, David Baldwin Jr., who had fought in the War of 1812. This brought some consolation, and charged my blood to do what I had to do for the Union. Our family had always been abolitionists, even running an underground railroad on my great uncle Ransom's farm in Atwater, Ohio. I remembered some of the events that had reached us in Logan County from Atwater that Ransom Baldwin was in the Independent Rifles since 1861 in the Civil War.

Underground Railroad- Home of Moses Baldwin

"When I had enlisted, I was not to leave until September, but the conflict had become so bad and the enemy so determined that it was necessary for me to go sooner. I left on the 15th day of August—only four days after I had enlisted. I was ordered to report to Fort Bellefontaine for training, but this had changed by the time we had arrived. This was such a surprise to me, and I was not ready, but I had put my name on the roll, and I could not go back on it.

"My wife had not been very well, but respected my decision, and she knew quite clearly that I could not make preparations as first planned, so I had to put my business in the hands of my father and Joseph, and then I left my dear wife there with my parents and my brother and his wife.

"After we all arrived by train in Bellefontaine, all enlistees were ordered to form a line at the train station. We watched loved ones, and friends, part with their young men. Wives and mothers were wringing their hands and crying in the bitterest grief, and teardrops were running down their furrowed cheeks, and the youth were sobbing as well. Fathers' prayers could be heard in the crowd, 'God bless our noble sons.' (As I pen these memories of the past, the tears fill my eyes, for the freshness of the memories of that war are but as yesterday.) On the sidetrack, there was a long train with the great American Flag streaming in the air with its emblem of freedom and American liberty—the great cause we were now to protect.

Ohio 96th Regiment Flag

"What had only seemed like moments to us later, we were now given to take the parting hand and receive the last kiss from many a dear wife and mother, and to hear father's last words that God would fight our battles for us and shelter us under his wings. These moments flew with the speed of time, and soon we heard the firm, but solace voice of the conductor, who seemed to enter into the spirit of the scene around him. He cried out, "All aboard" and then the shrill scream of the whistle, the sharp sound of break, and the great locomotive began to slowly move away. Handkerchiefs were waving from the tops of railroad cars as the wind caught them. They could be seen even as they became smaller. Then all was left to the thoughts of our sad hearts, and the lonely homes. (It is not by death alone that so frequently robs our homes, but it was the rebellious war, and it has always been rebellion that has robbed a home of its pleasure, even if we go back to the Garden of Eden.)

"Now we were in deeper thoughts as the engine plunged faster and faster along the iron bound railway as though she flew, but when the whistle blew at each crossing, she seemed to slow down. Then with a lunge of redoubled energy, she would pick up once again and rush along.

"Eight miles were now behind us, and soon we were in West Liberty and hearing the usual shout of the people that thronged the different railroad stations we had passed, 'Hurrah for the soldier boys. Hurrah for the boys in blue.' We passed Urbana, then direct to Camp Delaware where we were to make camp.

Camp Delaware under construction, circa 1891

"On the evening of the 15th of August, and for the first time we had tried our hand at preparing our meals. We had been furnished with baker's bread, coffee, and some meat, and a few other things that made our supper. After supper we gathered bushels of bread. We all lay down: some on the flour sacks, some on makeshift beds, but some tore around all night.

"The next morning, the 16th of August, we arose, ate breakfast, and then marched about a mile to the place where we were to encamp. After a few days passed, and we had been mustered in, I got word that my wife was very sick. So I reported to headquarters to see if I could go home to check on her. An officer gave me a pass to collect a furlough, and I went home where I found my wife in a very critical condition. My leaving so suddenly must have brought on the miscarriage, and it had nearly taken her away. She got better, and shortly I left her in the care of my mother who was very tender to her, for I had to return to camp.

"Camp Delaware was located nearly a mile east of the city on the banks of the Olentangy River or what is known as the big whetstone, for it is a very swift running stream with a rocky bottom. There were springs of different kinds of water that helped compose this great river. The White Sulfur Springs were near there, and in one of the springs there was a large stone that had been cut like an iron kettle with a hole in it the size of a man's foot, and the water came up through the middle, and where the water came up, it would fill this kettle looking stone. Anyway, the water is said to be very healthy. I will return to camp narrative.

"The duties of camp life consisted, in part, of cooking, drilling, standing guard, washing dishes, and once a week we had to wash our clothes, and that was a new line of business to us, but this all had been a long road without turns."

One of the first difficulties for a new recruit was to adapt to the army regimentation. Caring for personal needs, learning how cook rations or forage for food. They were taught how to help prevent scurvy, typhus, and other diseases, and to recognize bad water, and how to prevent poor sanitation.

Heavy equipment included a knapsack, haversack, canteen, and they had to carry rations for three days. They had a woolen blanket, shelter tent, winter clothing, tin cup and plate, knife, fork, spoon, stationery or journal, Bible, tobacco, pipe, comb, brush, and other essential items. As they entered battles, many discarded some of these items preferring to wear and keep only essentials. In the Civil War, shoes became extremely needed because they wore out quickly as the foot soldiers marched from battle to battle. This was true for both the Union and Confederate soldiers.

"Camp life was short to us, for in just several weeks, we had been ordered to prepare three-days rations, and to prepare to move out, but we knew not where we were going. As soon as due preparations were made, and provisions prepared, we were ordered to strike tents, and pack up. We were ordered to fall-in and soon enough, we saw the colonel in dress parade uniform march out with his sword at his side, and the captains were all in dress uniforms. We boys, eight in a line, with minds as much bewildered as a flock of sheep that were driven to slaughter, at least according to their knowledge of affairs. All of us at-ease and ready in line, when we heard the cry of the colonel, 'Attention battalion. Forward, march.' The 127th Regiment of Ohio moved off slowly and singing the words 'Delaware, in

Delaware, Union soldiers we became...' We were convinced that we were to leave the people of Ohio to go into business for certain in the South. I was in the 96th Regiment, Company H, we sometimes had trained together.

The 127th Regiment, formed as the Ohio Volunteer Infantry, had trained about a mile from Camp Delaware. They were the first African American unit of the Union Army and mustered in for three years of service on August 29, 1862 under the command of Colonel Joseph W. Vance. This was eighteen days after Stephen signed papers for enlistment.

In November of 1863 the regiment was re-designated the 5th United States Colored Infantry Regiment, and it moved to Norfolk, Virginia.

127th Ohio Infantry

Camp Delaware 1862-1864

THE WAR EXPERIENCES

"When passing the streets on our way to the depot, we heard the greetings of the people who lined the streets on both sides. Their words were again, "Goodbye soldiers, goodbye." Some gave us a card with their addresses, others shook our hands, and some were crying. Many followed us down to the train station where there stood a long train of cars waiting for us to get aboard with a multitude of people now everywhere.

"Soon the train began to move slowly away as a general cheer of the bystanders echoed in the air. We were on our way to the great city of Cincinnati.

"When we landed in Cincinnati, we were greeted again with the usual cheer.

"We immediately formed into line and marched to the wharf on the Ohio River where we boarded a steamboat that ferried us across the river into Kentucky. It was here that many of us realized that we were in one of the seceding states, at least in part, and it began to dawn on many of us that we had not ever been out of our native State of Ohio. We went a short distance to a hall where we took up our quarters. We were Company H, and it was here that we learned our first lessons in provost duties. I was frequently stationed at a landing of one on the ferryboats. Here I had found that it took some sacrifice to be a true soldier.

"While on duty one day, there was a man who had come up to me and gave a bill that was on the State of Indiana, and he asked me what it was. I told him that it was a dollar bill. He said, 'Will that bill be good enough for you to take me across the river?'

I said, 'Sir, I am not for sale, and you cannot buy a ferry across the river.' He left and returned in about an hour in a government wagon, he had changed his clothes, but the captain of the ferry said that this man must not go over, for there were orders that no more persons could be allowed over the state line north. There were so many going north to avoid the Kentucky draft. Then the man picked up a stone and said that he would knock the cap off of my head. I said that I would shoot him if he did not throw the stone down, so he dropped the stone and went away, and I never saw him again.

"We remained stationed in Covington for about two weeks in which time we learned about some of the indignity of the city, and the perils of the times of war. Many times we could hear the sound of feet of those who were fleeing from the police, and it had not been uncommon to hear the report of pistols in the chase.

"About this time, there were rumors of the approach of the noted Rebel Colonel John Morgan who had been breaking through the Union ranks, and in a dash he would do considerable harm by stealing and murdering, and then like a coward he would run again with his band of rebels.

"We were now ordered to move, and we went up the Ohio River about five miles and encamped at a place called Beechwood. (It was here that a turning point in my life occurred. I had been a strong hearty man who was able to do almost anything that such a strong man was capable of.) We were still looking for the approach of Morgan, but his scout had seen us, and he took his men around us to the west and north and made an attack on Fort Mitchell. We could see the fire from the canon, and could hear some of it, but it did not last long. In that skirmish, several of our Union soldiers had been wounded, yet a number of Morgan's men were killed and wounded. (Eventually Colonel Morgan was killed at Greeneville, Tennessee on 4 September 1864 when a surprise attack had been made against him and his men.)

"Here, I said was the turning point in my life. We had been stationed on an outpost guard. I was detailed with others of our small group to go about five miles up the Ohio River on the Kentucky side to watch some roads that came together from various parts of Kentucky, but also to check out some dangerous homes. We marched out through a rain and lay all night in our wet clothes, and I took a cold.

"The next night, the officer of the guard was making his rounds, and he had managed to slip in while boys were sleeping, and took their guns. They were afraid that they would get a bad report in the morning, so they came to me for help. He tried to take my rifle, but failed. Soon after, the two boys came to me and told me that the officer of the guard was fast asleep above us a short distance."

At night, the officer in charge of the soldiers would test them because of the fact that an enemy could sneak up on them and take their weapons. So during training it was protocol for the officer in charge to see if he could act as the enemy and confiscate their weapons without their knowing it. In the morning, the rifles that had been confiscated would be stood up in a row to show which soldiers failed the test. Those soldiers would then be punished with extra duties.

"I seized the opportunity to put a veto to his report for the next day. I cautiously approached him for I knew that I must be remarkably quiet, or I'd awaken him, he'd find out my plan, or he might shoot me in his hostile excitement. As I crawled near his tent, I could hear him snoring, so I inched my way to his side and knelt above him, so that I could clench his shoulders down if he had awakened before I had accomplished my objective. I removed his sword, which was my original intention. As I removed his sword from the scabbard, he moved a little, so I waited and breathed uneasily until he got still. Then I crawled backwards until I was out of his tent. Well, I had accomplished my deed, and that had been to stop his report in the camp. I know that I could have been court-martialed, but the boys had enough to think about. Many quietly thanked me the next day.

Someone found the officer's sword under a wagon, and the matter was closed."

Had Stephen been caught taking the officer's sword, he would have been court martialed. He did this so that the officer did not file a negative report against his comrades.

"The next day was a day of rest for us, so I thought I would write some letters to my friends at home. The Kentucky sun was high, and the rays of the autumn sun had been pouring down upon us, and my clothes, being still wet, I took them off to hang awhile on branches, and wrote to my friends. As I wrote my letters, I had become blind so that I could not see the lines on the paper. I waited awhile for I had felt very bad, and my head had such a strange feeling. It seemed to pass. I could see again and commenced to write, but I took another spell that was worse than the first. I had become weakened and could not write any more. I pulled myself together and reported to the doctor who said that I had sunstroke.

"The next morning orders came to strike the tents and to move out. They pulled the tent over me and left me stretched out on the ground in the hot sun. I was not able to help myself, but the regiment moved toward Covington. Those of us in our company who had fallen ill were left behind to do the best we could. We got up to do whatever we could, gathered our personal items, and in a short while, we started after our company that had gone ahead of us, with what little strength we had, and eventually traveled the five miles and caught up with them in Covington in the early afternoon. We were told to wait there until later. Then in late afternoon an express-man picked us up in his express wagon to take us to his house on a back street where he and his family lived. He introduced us to his wife, and well, I thought that she was one of the noblest women and nice to us. The express-man said to her, 'Sally, prepare the best meal that you have in the house for these soldiers, and I will prepare another team and wagon to take them to their regiment, and I will see why these soldiers were treated like this.'

"She got a splendid supper for us all, and then we all ate. The express-man came back in the house, after he had pulled his wagon in the front of the house. He told us to come out and to get into the wagon, and off we went in a rapid pace. We drove very fast most of the time, and it was in the middle of the night, and that had concerned us. We reached the regiment about midnight, but the express-man couldn't find the officer he had been looking for. On the other hand, an officer came to give us orders. We were immediately sent back to Covington's 11th Street hospital.

Union stationery from Fort Covington

LETTER TO ELLEN ON SEPTEMBER 18, 1862:

Dear wife, I received a letter from you this afternoon, and you cannot tell how glad I was to hear from you. You said that you were very much discouraged, but you must not be so, for the papers come here every day and are bringing the best of news. We are gaining ground faster now than ever have; since the war commenced, they are fighting every day.

Another day has arrived, and I am well as usual. I have just come from Newport, and the news of the day is in our favor. I think the war will be over this winter, and some think it will be over by Christmas.

I was at the Ohio River the other day, and saw a man lying near the shore at the edge of the water. He was drowned, and was black with mortification. He looked as if he had been there two or three weeks. He was the most awful sight I ever saw. He was a soldier, and he has friends mourning him... he has gone the way of all the earth that we must all follow sooner or later.

Well I received a letter from my sister, Almira, and she said that the folks are all right as usual.

Ellen, you wanted me to get you a dress, but they won't let me go to town. Even if they would, I don't have enough money now for I lost a dollar today, and I must keep the rest for letters. This is a poor country here. I must go to drill.

There we are though drilling. We are on a very high hill, and the men have cut the timber down...Well I can see the Ohio River from here, and we can see the snake from town.

You said that you wanted me to try to get a discharge. It is utterly impossible for me to get a discharge. The colonel cannot give me one. I should have to get a field officer to sign a discharge and then send it to governor of Ohio, then it goes to the Secretary of War, and it would take four or five months and then they would not grant it. So you see it is of no use to try for the release... Stephen

Great Naval Battle Engagement off Fort Wright

LETTER TO ELLEN FROM FORT COVINGTON ON SEPTEMBER 23, 1862:

Dear wife, I received yours yesterday, O how glad I am to think that you love to write to me. I love to get letters from you. It found me well as can be. You wanted to know the date of your letters that I had received from you... I was glad to hear that you were able to ride around. I will stay at Covington this year, I want you to come and see me.

You say that you are sorry that I am in so much danger. I am not in as much danger as you think that I am or any part of this affair. I am very easy about the danger here. All I am uneasy about is what is going on at home, and my wife, for I could not do better for anybody else, just you Ellen. Keep all the letters I send to you, for maybe there will be something in them that I may forget...

I am some afraid you will be on the go so much that you will exert yourself, so that you will get sick. O Ellen take good care of yourself, both body and soul.

We have to drill about half the time. There was a soldier arrested for going to sleep while he was on picket guard, and he receives his sentence today. He may be shot, and we boys, I mean some of the boys might have to witness this terrible duty.

I must quit, so farewell.
Stephen
write soon

Dry all the fruit that you harvest. I hope to help eat some of it this winter.

LETTER FROM FORT COVINGTON SEPTEMBER 1862:

Dear wife, precious Ellen,

I got your letter last night... and it was a welcome to me, but I did not finish reading until this morning. Pain is not very bad, although I am able for duty. You cannot tell how much pleasure it gives me to read your letters. O how glad I was to hear that you were getting better.

There are a great many men here, and the hills are fortified so that we are not in a great deal of danger. There is no news more special... but there was a rumor that rebels were headed this way from Lexington...You said that you were going to come down here... Take good care of yourself, both body and soul, and may the Lord bless you is my prayer.

Stephen H. Baldwin

Write often. Don't wait for me to write.

"In the early afternoon of the next day, we were sent to Camp Dennison in Hamilton County, Ohio. I remained at Dennison Army Hospital for two months in what I call an invalid ward. I was in Ward 16 for eight weeks under the care of doctors. My once strong and active body had become a wreck with heart disease and nervous debility and other kindred complaints had become the result. For the first time in my life, I felt like an invalid."

The records show that even thirty-five years after this journal entry, he still felt like an invalid. Life continued to be difficult for Stephen who was no stranger to sorrows and bereavements due to the fact that three of his five children died.

LETTER FROM CAMP DENNISON ON 4 OCTOBER 1862:

Dearest wife, I received your letter a few minutes ago, and was glad to hear from you as I always am. I am so glad that you are able to go around and are gaining your farmed color. You said that you wanted me to come and see you, but there is an awful chance that I cannot get a furlough now, but there may be a chance after awhile to come on a furlough. You said that you were afraid that we should go to the Potomac River. I suppose I never shall see that place for there is enough to see now. So you need not be uneasy about that.

I was on picket last night, and there were two men who came to part of our picket. They were halted three times, and then the men ran into the fields. A boy shot at them, but missed. The same men returned, and were halted again, and they ran again. Then there were two shots made at them, but they were not hit...they were not seen any more.

This is Sunday, and there was a prayer meeting here last night. We had a good meeting, and a lively time. There was one man that was a sinner when he went to the meeting, and came away a converted soldier. Bless the Lord for what he is doing here.

Ellen, don't be in too big of a hurry about coming here to the hospital. Wait till we get better fixed. You have no idea if things are fine or not, so please take my advice and wait. You can come just as soon as we get situated, and things are better. All right? I will send word, so you may come. I want to see you very badly, but don't be uneasy about us going to Virginia. Don't set yourself up too much about it...the news is favorable, yet in all of the papers, the word of the people can cross the river, so I was told without a pass, they can get a pass any how if they must cross, and all citizens can. Soldiers are kept in close quarters, for they cannot get a pass for anything, not even to go to town.

You wanted me to write a long letter, but there is no news more than usual. You were uneasy you said about me lying out of doors. We have got good tents to stay in...

Stephen

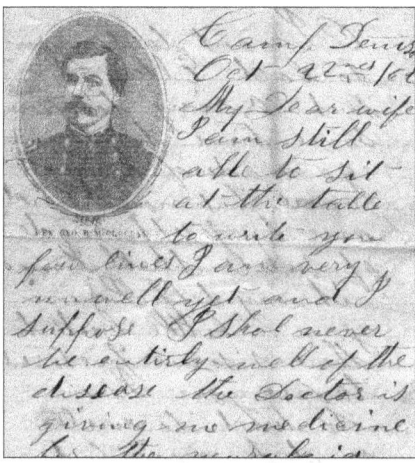

Gen. Geo. B. McClellan Stationery

LETTER TO ELLEN FROM CAMP DENNISON ON OCTOBER 22, 1862:

My dear wife,

Pain is still present, but I am able to sit at the table to write you a few lines. I am very much not well yet, and I suppose that I shall never be entirely well from the disease. The doctor is giving me medicine for the neurological condition, but it seems that he can do me no good yet. O you cannot tell how I was disappointed when I found that you did not come with Joseph. O I want to see you so badly. I sent you a ring some time ago made of cannel coal, but I sent another ring with Joseph that I had made myself of misele shell. I also sent you a little book.

There are some uncertain futures to face you.

I am too tired to write much now, but Joseph can tell you all about the news you will be able to hear, as well as in the other letters. O if I could just see you, I could talk so much more than I can write, but I must close for now by sending you my love and many prayers... I will never expect to be as stout as before I went to the war... so no more for now.

Stephen H. Baldwin

LETTER FROM CAMP DENNISON 27 NOVEMBER 1862:

Dear Wife,

I received your letter that had been written the 23rd. It was found in my bed, but I am not there now, for I am in pain some. The letters this morning did not come because of the rain, and that is the reason that I had received nothing yesterday. The doctor gave me quinine and...morphine, and it was not too strained and close, for [in awhile] he said that if my situation was not so strong, he would change the medicine again. Because I did not improve by the other day, he said that I was not fit to go to my regiment. So I shall not very soon go. I expect that they are going to discharge some, but not me, and I do not expect one soon, if ever. The doctors are so slow. I have gotten what the doctors call Neuralgia. This is pain in nerves in my right arm and in the right side of my head. This pains me so. I can hardly write. I went out the other day and routed a rabbit. It ran some fifty yards and stopped; I followed after in carefully, but it ran a little way, and then I shot at it with my revolver and killed it. Harrison Sullivan ran up to it. The rabbit limped over on a chunk of wood, and he picked it up and brought it to the camp. The cooks that cleaned it had kept all the fat and choice cuts, the way the civilians do. These cooks are no better than thieves.

Well I cannot tell when pay day will be yet, but as soon as I get my money, I will send it so that you can come, if you are able to, and if there is nothing to do with me, that is the discharge, and I can go home. If they don't do anything with me after I get my pay, I will go to the regiment to get a discharge. I can get one by going there, for there had been some desertions in the 96th, and many got discharges and have gone home. So if they don't do anything with me after I get my money, I will go to the regiment and try it.

Ellen, I want you to write to me about all the news of the country, and especially about your health. There are things I would write about, if I dare, but you know how to write anyhow. So write and let me know all.

Tell Nancy that her letter has gone to Morrison Baldwin.

Now Ellen, be very careful with yourself. I am not thinking of any more too wise about you. O yes, today is Thanksgiving Day, so let us give thanks to the Lord for his goodness and his mercies. Pray that he will help us, and keep us from danger. This is the prayer of your loving husband, Stephen Baldwin.

I forgot to tell you of the accident. There was a man walking on the railroad tracks, and the trains were going both ways, and he didn't see the one, and he was drunk. One of the trains slowed and tried to warn him with his whistle, but it struck him, but it did not kill him. He was bruised very badly.

[Neuralgia is a sharp, shocking pain due to irritation or damage to the nerve. It was very difficult for soldiers who suffered from this disorder because the pain could occur while the soldier was in hand-to-hand combat, or perhaps while firing a rifle and missing the target. Once diagnosed with this disorder, the soldier was typically not permitted to go back into combat.]

LETTER SENT TO ELLEN FROM CAMP DENNISON 2 DECEMBER 1862:

Dear wife,

I have devoted myself to write a few lines to let you know the turn of my fortune. There is good news for our regimental surge and the situation here in camp tonight. They are wanting to recruit some new men, and those that are not able to do duty will be discharged sooner than they, the new recruits, will be here in camp. So be in good cheer, for I think that we will get home now before long. We will start for Memphis, Tennessee, so I think that old Tennessee won't hold us long. I feel better in spirit, but not in body. I am better satisfied than I was in the morning.

If you get this before Peter comes back, I want you to keep my boots there till I come home. Now, don't think that I have gone so far that I cannot come home, for I have not, but I can come home in three days after I start. Well, I shall get to see some of the country and get to come home before long. When you write the next letter, send it to Memphis, Tennessee in care of Capt. Neven, Company H, 96th Regiment.

Tell Jonah that I shall see Morrison sooner now. Tell all that you see, that I am well, and I am glad of it. All the 96th that are able to walk around are forming a squad.

Ellen, tell Joseph that that song is only partly my composition. I am going to send some things home by express to Bellefontaine. It will be sent in Joseph's name. There will be a blanket for father. Well, I cannot think of anything more tonight. So fare well from your loving husband. Take care of yourself now, and remember that my prayers are always going up for you.

        Stephen H. Baldwin

"About a month later, I was surprised on an afternoon when my dear wife Eleanor and my brother Joseph came to Camp Dennison. There were several of our neighbors who also were here: Peter Paris, Clark Ibonvoorhis, Harrison Sullivan, and Charlie Wigus, and a cousin to my wife, Elisha Dobbins. These visits seemed to bring a bit of life and strength back. While my brother was with me at the camp, we went walking one day, and we found the mayor of a nearby town shooting quite a distance at targets. As we approached him, I had noticed that the rifle looked to be a new type of rifle. He was shooting at a mark about a hundred yards off. I asked him if I might shoot once, and he said that I might. I made the shot steady on that clear day and hit the paper marker. He told me that that was the best shot of the day. As I walked back, I thought what a great rifle that would be for our boys.

"I had been in the camp hospital for eight weeks, and the days were humdrum which had been irksome to me. Once I was permitted to go home on what we termed a breach. That is, we went home without a pass, for our ward master did the answering of the roll call for us until we returned. Thus, several of us got to see our friends once more. I enjoyed the trip real well because I was able to see my wife again, my parents, and others, but the joy came to an end when I had to return to camp.

"I had grown so tired of my camp life that I resolved to go and hunt my regiment. About the 15th of December 1862, I left Camp Dennison to hunt for the boys of my own company. I first went to Cincinnati where I had found information as to where my regiment had been stationed. I went to headquarters and got several day's rations and a pass to Memphis, Tennessee. I was told to get a mail packet at the dock before boarding.

"I and several other boys went down to the wharf where we had found the mail packet, and we were ready to start down the Ohio River to Cairo, Illinois where we would pick up the Mississippi River. Several of us got on board, for we all were looking for our regiment. We moved off down the Ohio enjoying ourselves the best we could, and that went real well with the boys who had been so sick for so long. The air was pure and the weather fine. The boat's usual trip was to New Orleans, but communications were cut off, for the rebels had control, so she could not even go as far as Fort Vicksburg. In late afternoon, we had to maneuver through the locks that had been built about thirty to forty years ago, and this was because the Ohio River was too low at times. In fact, there are times that people could walk across the mighty Ohio River on dry ground.

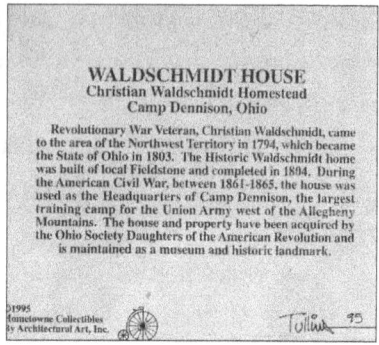

Camp Dennison Replica

Replicas of Camp Dennison are made and sold by the *Daughters of the American Revolution* who raised money to restore the buildings.

A steamer going through locks on the Ohio River used to transport Union troops.

"We got through the locks at sunset. We moved down river to the little town of Hudson on the Kentucky side where we anchored. Early the next morning they hoisted anchor, and we again started down the great river that began to show signs of being deeper, for the waters ran more smoothly. Soon we saw the Wabash River on our right entering the Ohio River. From there we went straight to Cairo, Illinois where we landed and took some refreshments. Then we left the Ohio River and floated out on the bosom of the mighty Mississippi River at the rate of eight miles an hour. We saw wild geese, ducks, and other things on the surface of the water. One of the boys who had an Army rifle, shot at a flock of wild geese that were flying near the river that seemed to be a mile away, but he of course missed, and I saw the ball hit the water with a little splash, and then skip up that made the flock dodge apart. We did have some sport after all, shooting at things on the water as they passed by. We did enjoy the ride very well.

"My health began to improve a little as I stood on the deck watching the country as it passed by us. This was new to me, and I believe that kept my mind from thinking about my condition.

"The river was getting up, for there had been heavy rains west and north of us. The banks were caving in, and the trees that stood near the edge would frequently fall in with the tops hitting the water. The timber seemed to be mostly cottonwood. Once we scared an old bruin, and when he saw the boat, he scampered his brown wet fur as fast as he could into the woods. Thus, we sported our way until we reached Memphis, Tennessee where our regiment was stationed at the time. Memphis is situated on a rising piece of country, and is a rather beautiful location. The ground sloped downward toward the courthouse where there were plenty of squirrels skipping about on all sides of me as I passed along. They were near enough that I had to gently kick them out of the way. As I passed down another street to the soldier's home, I heard the crack of a gun off to the right of me, and immediately the ball passed so near me, I could hear the whistle of it as it went cutting through the air. In the morning I heard that a man had been shot the night before, so I supposed that the same ball passed through the man's body, killing him. I stayed home that night and went to the regiment in the morning.

"I found the boys well and cheerful, and they were glad to see me. Here I began to improve, for it was a healthy place and the water was good. We were there two days when we got orders that we must move. The next night we were surprised by a false alarm. I had not been given my rifle since I had returned. I was in my tent preparing some balls for my revolver (as it was a loose ammunition piece), when we heard the long roll of a volley. That meant business at once. Perhaps it was the approaching enemy. Every man went to his gun and me to my revolver. I put in the five shots, and got in line about as quick as anyone who had strapped on their gun. This was just after dark, but soon we found it to be a false alarm. A soldier had been killed a day ago, and had a late evening burial ceremony, and the color guard shot off three volleys over his grave.

"The morning after this excitement, we joined a naval fleet and got on board of the Hiawatha and went further down the Mississippi. We left Memphis about the 18th of December on board of this great steamer. She was one hundred and twenty feet long, and sixty feet wide. We took our quarters in the stern where we lay day and night, wet or dry, for it mattered not about the cold or wet. We were in it just the same and had to stick to our quarters. We were not there to complain."

USS Rattler, a Union tinclad gunboat – a typical steamer used in the Civil War.

"We ran down the Mississippi with nothing of note, till we had come to Island No. 10 where our boat held up, so we could see the ravages of the battle that had been fought there, and the affect it had on the surroundings. At least the troops had gone from the field of battle. There were a great number of things to see, such as trees that had been cut off by cannon balls ten to forty feet high. It looked somewhat like a terrible storm, like a tornado had gone through, but the sun was shining and everything was plain to see: the rifle pits, Quaker's graves still there, and a lot of debris. All of this showed again the horrors of war.

"We left Island No. 10, but soon had halted above a little town where a few months before a colored man and a school teacher had been put in a hog-head, a kind of large barrel, and thrown into the Mississippi River to drown them both. The teacher had been an abolitionist. No sooner had we pulled the boat to shore, that the boys made for the town, for revenge had filled their hearts because of what they had done to these two people. They also wanted to pay them for the destruction we had witnessed earlier. With their Northern abolitionist blood boiling, they made a straight shot for town. Soon there was black smoke that arose from different storehouses. We had some difficulties, but shortly after, an officer eventually restrained us, but not until the most part of the village was in ashes. The village paid dearly for their so-called "fun" that did them no good. We were too late to save the young man who had been a teacher, nor the colored man.

"We got aboard and were ordered down the river. On our southbound journey we had seen quite a number of rebel prisoners that had been taken in other places. They were going north for safekeeping. They looked very rough in their walnut brown clothes, but pleasure was not the object of our trip, nor was there any fun in it. In a few days we found a battle.

"We kept moving on the river until we came to the mouth of the Yazoo River, so named by La Salle, the French explorer. The waters looked like ink, and it was poison to us, and it was very much against my health, as my health had been declining again. In fact, I felt much worse, especially living on the deck of the steamer.

"We went up the Yazoo about twenty-five miles to a large slave plantation. We dropped anchor, landed, and the boys were ordered to form a line, but I was not included, neither were twenty-four other soldiers who remained with the boat because none of us were well.

"The next day, about the 27th or 28th of December, we were out on deck and listening to the battle. We could hear the thunder of canon fire, the rolling of musketry, and a sense of solemnity came over us. We began to reason that maybe the boys were in a hot battle and a few of us might tip the scale in our favor, so we began to devise a means of getting to them. There was a picket line between them and us so that privates could not pass. While we were contriving as to how we could help, Major McElroy came along, and we asked him to take us through the line, and he kindly said that he would. We made ready and started to pick our way through these bayous. Some were quite deep and inhabited by alligators. We finally arrived at the picket line, and the sergeant in charge passed us through. We were surrounded with Cyprus timber and canebrake in these dense woods. The density and loneliness would almost make a squirrel lonely, except for the heavy thunder of the artillery, and the constant roar of musketry made it more *doleful. We looked up above the bank of the river to see a dead moose that hung from a large limb with a bright gray collar that made it gloomier. It was the flats of the year, and we could see where the high waterline had been about fifteen feet above our heads. We went about a mile in the thicket, and found our boys who were being held back in reserve for a charge on the enemy's rifle pits. While we lay there, a constant rain fell, until we were drenched. The mud that we had picked up in the river was now a soppy red. As I lay there with all the men, I thought about what it would be like to have a hundred head of cattle in a pen out of doors when it is raining, and they have been tramping around in the mud; think of putting a blanket down for them to sleep on. Well, I broke the vine that we call the bittersweet, and lay there all night with my legs lopping in the mud.*

"Early the next morning, I got up and walked around to see the fighting, and one of the rebs came and took a shot at me, but he missed his aim. I just thought that he was a poor shot or a poor marksman. I thought that I could have done better with my six-shooter. Anyway he kept close for a while.

"Later when I had been eating my rations while sitting beside a tree with one of the boys, a ball struck the tree between our heads, but fanned one side of my head blowing the hair away from my ear. My friend dodged left when the ball hit the tree and spilled his coffee, and it burned him. He said with a smile, that he would rather that they be more careful and not bother him when he was eating his dinner. We had a couple of days like this with sniper fire or a reb just trying to take out a Yankee.

"The next day was January 1, 1863, and on this memorable day to many, about dusk we could see that something was going on in the profound silence. The officers finally came over to us and said that there must not be any loud talk, and we could see the artillery going toward the open fields. After dark we got the word in a whisper to get in line. Then we received an order in a whisper, "Forward march." We moved out over the brush and logs until we had come in sight of the open fields. I had stayed with them up to the edge of the woods, but I could go no further, for I had no rifle. They had to leave me there alone, and moved out several yards, but I was not there alone for long for rebels were soon in the

woods—in all directions. I quickly got under a white thorn bush and thought I would do best for myself. I didn't think that they would look in a thick thorn bush. I had my revolver which I knew I could use to a good advantage, for I knew that I could get six of them while they only got one of me. I was there a while, and a thorn or two had poked through my uniform, but they soon left the woods, and I carefully crawled out from under that prickly bush with a few scratches. As I stood, I saw a small light in the distance. I moved slowly watching every step. The light was on one of the main masts of the boat. How I got through without getting bogged down one of those bayous, I can never tell. I suppose that the alligators knew more, but were not that hungry. I got to the boat just as the rear end of the regiment was getting aboard. I now felt very relieved. All of our regiment that had been used for a backup, made it back. A navy officer told me that the Yazoo River had claimed many of our steamers in last year.

"After those previous cold and wet nights, I was getting worse. The regiment officers didn't force the sick to do anything above their physical capabilities. We often did more than they had expected, and of course, they appreciated that under these awful conditions.

LETTER TO ELLEN ON JANUARY 2, 1863 FROM THE STEAMER HEADING TO ARKANSAS:

Dear wife,

After being on the boat for several days, I started out to see what the boat was doing. In the woods, when I got here, I was found in the line of battle expecting every inmate to be called up to fight, but we were lucky. We have not had to fight any yet, but I have seen it done for the Rebels, for they were shooting our Union boys and our boys were shooting the rebels. I saw several men dead lying on the battle field. There was one that crossed a bayou when there was 500 shots at him, but they all missed him. We are now on the boat.

When you had heard from me, there was one who had died here the day before yesterday in Co. H, 96 Reg. We are now on the Yazoo River today and expect to leave soon.

This is the 4th day on the boat, and we are on the Mississippi, and headed up the river, but where we are going I cannot tell, but at least we got out of the woods on the Yazoo River. I am now quarantined.

I am about the same state of health as before. Well, Ellen, My dear wife, I got your letter this morning, and O how glad I was to hear from you. You wanted to know where I would find land, so as to buy 10 acres with the money I have. There are lots of it in close by and lots of it in Ohio, and lots of it in Indiana that I can get for 5 dollars per acre. So you may know that I am going to have some land if ever I get home safe.

There is one thing certain, and that is, if the officers of this regiment do not do better than they have been doing, I will take a trench and never return to the regiment again. I can, but if I do I will take you with me. I do not expect to desert, if I can help it. There are lots of boys that would go if they had half the chance. The regiment is getting some deserters. If I try it, they will not get me, for I will go to Canada where the colored men are free. Then they can whistle and fight it out themselves.

Well, I would like to have the news this morning. There are boats lying all along the river…

It has been a month since I had heard from you. O Ellen, do write often for you have a chance to write oftener than I have. You do not know how bad I want to see you, my loving wife, the only hope for earthly happiness.

From your loving husband,
Stephen H. Baldwin

[*This was added to the letter above written to Ellen.*]

Well Nancy, I have got your letter today. The reason I have not written more to you is because Ellen has been getting letters, so you can hear from me. Well the boys have gone out on the shore, and set a house on fire. There are several houses there, and I expected they will all be burned. It makes a big fire. You said you wished that I was there to learn arithmetic. I wish that I was as bad as you do, so no more at this time Nancy Miller.

"In the morning of the 2nd of January, we sailed back to the Mississippi, then north to Arkansas. We had heard that this was to be a critical battle, and that put us thinking the worse. We were heading to the Arkansas Post or Fort Hindman, a rebel fort where we were to have the memorable Battle of Arkansas on the 9th through the 11th of January 1863. We heard that more than two hundred and fifty Texans had come to fight with the other rebs. We had several Union gunboats in the Arkansas River that bombarded the fort most of the night of the 10th. Our boys joined others to attack the post, but it was the U. S. Navy gunboats that sealed their fate that cold snowy night, with as much as six inches of snow.

Union Gunboats on the Arkansas River

Battle scene at Camp Arkansas/Fort Hindman

The Union and Confederate forces fought vigorously for two days. This victorious battle for the Union Army set the necessary stage for the Union Army and Navy to take back Vicksburg, Mississippi. Union Maj. Gen. John A. McClernand's loss in the 96th Regiment was ten men killed, and twenty-six were wounded. The 96th Regiment was then sent to Young's Point, Louisiana, and the siege of Vicksburg began 22 May 1863 and concluded 4 July 1863.

"The next day after the battle, I saw that the gunboats had gotten up near the fort with their loaded canon fire. I went out to look over the work of death which is a common result of war. I went first to see the inroads that our own company first made. The wounded had been cared for, but the dead were still there, everywhere. The first one that I saw was U. B. Sesler, one of our own men. He had received a ball a little to the outside of his left forehead. The ball passed almost in a center course through the brain—he was dead instantly. (Here again I paused to think of U.B., for he was a wild young man and could out swear most men)... I saw several of our Union boys of the 96th Regiment cold in death. I had not seen this much death before. This left me saddened beyond words.

"Then I went over to the rifle pits to see the work done on the other side of the hill. I must describe the entrenchments around the fort. It surely had not been made secure as they had thought. The ditch around the fort was about six feet deep and six feet wide, and the dirt had been thrown up in a bank on the inside next to the fort, so that no one could jump across it to the fort, for it was near ten feet high. Then in the bottom part of the bank the rebels had driven stakes into the ground that had been sharpened to a point. Surely anyone attempting to jump over this defense, and failed, would be killed, but notwithstanding, after the bombardments since the 9th and 10th, we scaled the battered walls, and took the fort and almost 4,000 prisoners. Inside the fort was a great slaughter. I saw men in almost all disfigured shapes, some with their heads torn off, or legs and arms mangled or torn off. Before entering, I saw a rebel torn to strings and thrown out of the entrenchment by the bursting of a shell and landed on a pile of brush. One man had been torn open, and I could see his heart and liver. I looked around more, yet found so many dead. My mind had a hard time taking this all in. This was the curse of slavery... in America. When the south held in chains the colored race, it was cursed.

"I went to the front of the fort that faces the Arkansas River where there were two guns that run a one hundred and thirty-two pound ball. A Union gunboat that was one mile down the river had disabled one of the guns. The fort had been made of old fashioned flat railroad railing that had been placed close together, so as to have large balls glance off and go over the fort, but the gunboat canon ball went right through this fortification as though they had been made of pinewood. The splinters flew so that this sometimes killed the rebels. They could not move from their two guns because sharp shooters would pick them off every time. (When I look over these things in my mind, I am compelled to say, 'O, the cruelty of war. O Satan thou art the culmination of evil, for thou art the enemy of every good.') [Stephen was a minister at this time in the diary.]

"The soil was not good here, and there were some small white oak trees growing on the knoll. Across the river there was good timber and canebrake in abundance. None of nature's beauty found here could conceal any of the death of war. I gathered my thoughts as I returned to the steamer.

"I was tired now, for I felt quite poorly, for the chronic diarrhea was now working on me in addition to heart disease that was the result of my sunstroke that came upon me in Kentucky. At the steamer the boys and I got on board, for we were to guard prisoners and take them north. There were a lot of dusky looking fellows who seemed half starved, so we threw some crackers to them from our boat. As they passed near us, they would holler for more. They were poorly clad, and the cold morning made it worse for them. Some of them would not make it to the prison camps in the North.

Lady Liberty Standing with flag

LETTER SENT TO ELLEN FROM THE STEAMER ON THE MISSISSIPPI RIVER JANUARY 7, 1863:

Dear wife,

I received your letter day before yesterday and was glad to hear from you. Your letter found me no better. I have been very sick for awhile, but I have gotten better. We are still on the steamer on the Mississippi River in sight of Jackson, Missouri…but I am rather sick and have gone to the hospital. Well you wanted to know what sort of a bed I had. I have a tent with weeds on the ground and an oil clothe blanket on that. Morrison and I put our blankets on that and covering with them. Our victuals are not good nor plenty. The river is rising every day. I have sold my revolver to Morrison. He gave me 19 dollars at pay day, and a watch.

I have a pretty bad cough.

I am out of stamps, so I shall have to send for some, or send my letters without stamps.

I have had a gathering in my head, and it is not quite well. I have suffered a great deal for some time back, but I am better now. I am out of ink. I wish I had some ink powders. We have not got our pay yet, and don't know when we will have it.

Ellen, write all the news, and write long letters as you can. You need not look far. I have not had a chance down here to write, so you must excuse me, and don't look for me home till I come. So, my paper is out and I must close by sending my love to my wife Eleanor, from Stephen H. Baldwin.

"January 13, 1863 was a memorable day to me. After lying in the snow, I began to go downhill a bit. My health was not quite as good as I had thought that it might be as we were heading north.

"Our boat returned to the Arkansas River and back to the Mississippi River, and headed south then we pulled up to what was called the Milliken's Bend. It was a short curve in the river on the Louisiana side. We made camp here. I was very sick by this time, and made slow progress getting away from the boat. I got on the ground, and went a few yards, and then lie down on the ground and put my head on my knapsack for a pillow. I got up and soon lie down again as before until the doctor came that way, and he sent me to a field hospital that was in Young's Point. The doctor gave me something, and told me to get rest. That was not going to help much, but soon that afternoon, I was back with my regiment.

"After all that sickness, we came up the Mississippi in the last week in January. How long it took us, I do not know, but I think we stopped at Young's Point, but I am not sure, for I was so sick, and I had a gathering in my head. During the trip up the river, I had to lie on the ground, and I had to leave the steamer often to go into the woods. The boys were now getting sick, and many died. The field hospital that we were heading for had been a dwelling house, and the occupants had gone, for war had driven them away. When we docked, I was sent to that house that was used for a field hospital.

"I do not know how long I had been there, for I was sick neigh unto death. I was there several weeks, and quite a good many other boys died. Few letters came, and I had not been able to write, for I was slow to getting better. I did not share everything about the war with my dear wife. She worried enough on that account.

"On the 23rd of March, while sitting up on a cot, an orderly who was a sergeant came up to see me, and I was real glad to see him even though I had not known his errand. When he had talked awhile, he took out some papers from his pocket, and asked me if I would like to go home. I, of course, said that I would. I did not know at the time, for I had thought that he had gotten me a furlough, but he said that I was not a soldier anymore, and the paper that he had in his hand, was my discharge. Then we talked awhile, and he bid me farewell and went his way. I sat there for a spell in almost disbelief, for I longed to see my family, and move on from the death of war.

"In the morning of March 26, 1863, about nine o'clock the ambulance drove up to take the two of us ill men a short distance to the boat landing. J. M. Baldwin and J. L Rochell came to help me get on the steamer. I got on board by these two boys getting under my arms and supporting me up the steps, and then they bid me farewell, and then they went back to the hospital.

I made a bed of my wool blanket and lay down. I now felt that I was my own man again, and while I write this almost thirty-five years since that time, I am still suffering from the visions of war."

On March 23, 1863, at Milliken's Bend, the Union Army Surgeon issued a certificate of disability to Private Stephen H. Baldwin. Milliken's Bend had been a staging area for General U. S. Grant for his attack on Vicksburg where he assembled 30,000 troops. It was a small town of two hundred people, two main stores, and a Catholic church. It was tragically washed away in a flood in 1880. To save the church, it was dismantled and moved to higher ground.

LETTER SENT TO WIFE, ELLEN, 26 MARCH 1863 FROM THE FIELD HOSPITAL:

Dear wife,

I'm pleased to be seated and able to write a few lines to you, to let you know how I am getting along. My pain is back on the side of my head and in my arm, and my heart is no better, but I have gained in the flesh a little. We were about to starve for the want of bread; so I began to steal a little from the commissary for some things, so we could trade meat for the bread. Also, I found a barrel that had molasses in it, so I went and got buckets for about a gallon and a half. Harmen Elliot got about half gallon, so we took that and traded it for bread. The man in charge of purchasing goods for the commissary said that he would give goods per gallon. So the molasses came to one dollar, and he mistakenly traded out ten dollars in bread. Wherefore, he soon noticed his mistake, but we took the bread away. We got ten dollars worth of bread for one dollar. You will keep that still about me stealing, for if it should get back here, I should be punished for it severely. The reason I was forced to do such wrongful acts is because the man who supplied our regiment with rations was shorting us 400 dollars worth of rations for his own gain.

I will now tell you what we are about to do. Sam Deardoff is making up dough to make a pot pie out of a beef head. Harmen Elliot is cooking the meat, and I am writing a letter to the only woman I ever loved.

Ellen, I wrote a month ago to you, and sent an order to the bank, for 100 dollars to buy you a pair of shoes, and a dress, and send a few dollars to me. If you remember, Father and Joseph have been putting money aside that they owed me for the work I did before I left for the war. You need not send any to me if you draw less. I shall draw some soon here from my pay. I sold my watch, and should get something on that as soon as the sutler comes (a civilian businessman who was permitted to come into a military camp during the Civil War with his wagon of goods).

Well, I must close for now, for I must write a letter to Almira and the rest of the family. So farewell for the present and may the good Lord keep you and protect you is my prayer.

Stephen H. Baldwin

All the soldiers remember "the boys" they left behind. Their comrades who became like brothers and friends while fighting side by side. Many of them wrote poems and songs about their service in the Union Army. A soldier from Stephen's regiment, wrote this poem:

"The Boys We Left Behind"
By Nathaniel D. Watkins,
Company A, 96th Ohio Volunteer Infantry

Old comrades of the Ninety-sixth
To all a hearty greeting;
With fervent grasp each hand we clasp
At this our yearly meeting.
We'll fight our battles o're again,
Though, sadly they'll remind
Us of many gallant men—
The boys we left behind

Scenes, long past, come flitting fast
O're memory's magic mirror,
And half-forgotten face grow
Upon us, nearer dearer.
We see, again, the weeping friends
As they, with tears, resigned us—
We see, again, those absent boys—
The boys we left behind.

RETURNING HOME

"Like I said, on the 24th of March 1863, the boat started north, up the river, but not before I had bid farewell to my comrades in the land of blood and war. There were nearly fifteen hundred miles that lay between my home and me. It was with great difficulty that I got through.

"After four days we landed at Memphis, Tennessee where I was able to draw my pay. After I got that business settled, and had my pay, I went back to the boat. I got back on the steamer just in time to watch my comrade who was sent with me, die after his parting blessing. I then made suitable arrangements for his burial, and put his business into the hands of the state agent. I again went back on board and started for home.

"The journey seemed very tedious to me, and I was very tired, and had no strength to run about and to enjoy the trip. I had to stay close because the red scurvy had set in with weakness, but not any trouble with my gums, for it made me feel worse in some ways, but in general I felt a bit stronger. On the first day of April, I went on shore at Cairo, Illinois. Here we had to wait several hours for the railroad cars, and then we got on board the car, and the ride seemed quite long. We arrived at Bellefontaine about 12 o'clock, on the third of April 1863. I stayed at my uncle Samuel Milligan's until the next day. A neighbor who lived next to my father's farm had come to town. I asked if I could get a ride back home, and he agreed. The buckboard he drove was somewhat of a comfort to me as my mind was busy thinking about my wife, family, and the farm. Soon I would hold her in my arms.

"I got home the 4th of April before dark. I had just been ten days on the road from the field house hospital to my father's home. I found friends well, but very much surprised to see me. I was like a dead man that rose from the grave, for they had heard about ten days before that I was dead and buried. When I walked up toward the house, I found my mother standing out on the south side looking for something. She heard the dog bark as though he knew someone was coming, so she came around to see. The little dog ceased to bark and trotted along before me as though to say, 'I'll go tell them you are coming.' When I spoke to Mother, she was so overcome that she couldn't speak at first. My wife, Ellen, heard my mother's excitement, and came rushing out, followed by my father. At once they were hugging me, kissing, and pawing, but I had to tell them, 'I must sit down.' They saw that I was just about too sick, and they grabbed under my arms, and helped me in the house. Mother was the first one in the house. She got a big armchair, with quilts and pillows, and pushed it in front of a large fire in the hearth, just as Ellen came back in from the back bedroom. I stood, and we embraced. She was actually holding me steady. I kissed her warm cheek, and held her for some time. I whispered in her ear, that I had long missed her tenderness. We all sat around the fire, as mother prepared something to eat. We talked very little about the particulars of war, for I was not up to it.

"My precious Ellen was feeling better, and my dear parents were doing well. Joseph and his wife had been working hard helping our parents with the farm.

"Later that evening, Father explained that the weather had been cool, and the sugar camp had not been closed up, and so they could still do some sugar making. We talked about the sugar camp which brought good memories of making syrup.

"After I had gained some strength, and in a few days, I went with them to the camp to make a fire for making our sugar. Memories came back of the days here before the war. When I think of 'before the war', it reminds me of it, and gathering starts in my head. The voices of my family, and doing the things I used to do, helped me.

"The last week in May, Father and Joseph told me that they had taken a large job of cutting railroad wood, and they wanted to hire me to split wood and cut drags to haul logs to our sawmill to cut into various planks of wood and railroad ties. They had owed me some money when I got married, before I went to the war, so I took the money at that time."

Unfortunately, Stephen's return did not provide him relief from the chronic illnesses he had developed while serving in the military. On 28 April 1863, he applied for a pension for chronic diarrhea which was considered an invalid classification. He also suffered from pain caused by Neuralgia, and the emotional problems caused by his diagnosis of having a "soldier's heart" which would be considered Post Traumatic Stress Disorder (PTSD) today. Medication for his physical and emotional illnesses had not yet been discovered and so he had to try to cope the best he could with the brutal effects of these problems.

> "My wife and I lived with my parents until the spring of the next year. After I got so that I could work a little, I went to my brother-in-law's to run his sawmill engine in the winter of 1863. In the spring of 1864, I rented a piece of land for corn, and raised a good crop for us mainly to save money."
>
> "I had lived in several places for short times before I got real stout. Then I moved onto a place where I expected some hostilities from the owners, and I was not disappointed, yet I stayed a year. My daughter Ella M. Baldwin was born on March 23, 1864.
>
> "My mother-in-law died in the winter of 1864. She left five children, and her husband was still in the war, but in 1865, my father-in-law died in the last battle of the war in Columbus, Georgia on April 16th, and soon five children came under my care. I had been appointed guardian of all but one of the children who was on his own. We did not have a child at that time of her passing, but by the time my father-in-law died, we had one child, making our family seven. Family cares in such times as these made life rather hard, but Ellen's siblings were able to help considerably. As the years passed, one by one her siblings married or went out on their own."

FARMING AND OTHER BUSINESSES

"I made some trades and some changes that brought us extra money, and I began to look for a future home for wife, daughter, and myself. I made a sale of all the property that I could spare, and turned it into a note of good faith for one hundred and seventy-five dollars. This, of course, included the money I had gotten from the government when I had been discharged. The $13.00 a month in the Union Army didn't go far, but it did help. I soon made a trade that made me tremble. I could not find a small piece of ground to buy, but then I was offered fifty acres at thirteen dollars and fifty cents per acre. When I signed the notes for $675.00, my hand trembled for fear that I could not pay out, and would lose all. Even neighbors had said that I would never be able to pay for it. I worked early and late, and saved all that I could, for about six years, and finally got a deed, clear of debt. During this time, I had built a little frame house on it. This place was in Union County, Ohio. We lived in this small old cabin for several years with Eleanor's siblings. They all pitched in with chores, and we were glad to share what we had with them.

"During these three years we had a son, Munson, who was born January 23, 1866, but Munson took the diphtheria after we moved into the house in the woods. He died on September 15, 1867. Our daughter, Melinda Bell, was born September 6, 1868.

"In early 1870, with our daughters Ella May, Melinda Bell, and two of Ellen's siblings, I bought a lot and built a house on it, even though I still owned the cabin and mill. Just before it was complete, it took fire and burned to the ground. I had four hundred dollars in the marble shop, where I had owned a share, and the house was a loss of more than a thousand dollars. In just a few months, I had lost about fifteen hundred dollars, and the trouble was not yet over. We had to move what little we had saved out of the fire, into another house. This house had to be papered before it was fit to move into, so we went to work at it, but it was a terrible job because there were nine thicknesses of paper on the walls. I worked on it with my wife for about six hours a day. We finally finished it and papered in about three days. We were finally getting settled in when the light of our home, Melinda took sick. We sent for Dr. Allen who had come to see her, but it did her no good, for he did not know what was the matter with her. I told him that I supposed it to be the scarlet fever, and he said, 'No it was not.' I asked him three times if he was sure that it was not the scarlet fever, and each time he replied, 'No, but I do believe that the child will die.' After that he left, but told Darling, the Post Master that it was the old fashioned scarlet fever, and that she would die. The same day, she died, and again our home seemed broken up. Our grief was almost too much for us. Our home was reduced to Ell, Ella, and me—one child again. Our year old son, Munson, and now Melinda were gone. Poor little Melinda died on April 3, 1870. Burying these little ones brought death around me again. Dear Eleanor kept us together. It seemed we had our share of sorrows that looked as if it was to merely bring more living expenses, and our living expenses were just enough to make it in our new place. Many a time we felt our dependence on Him who even feeds the ravens when they cry. Yet, in all my despair and worry, the Lord prospered us, and we paid off the land debt. Soon I was in a position to buy twenty acres more, and traded part of the fifty acres on half interest in a new sawmill. I was successful in the mill and made money so that I was able to buy out the other share. I ran the mill for about eight years with more success. I liked being my own boss again. During these years, we enjoyed life as far as the blessings of God are concerned. Our family that included Ellen's siblings who were growing, but two of the four children had married, and the others remained with us. Also at this time, my parents sold out the old place, and moved into my place, but I had purchased the place on which my mill stood, and that money provided for the expansion of the cabin, and the room we needed for my parents.

"It was kind of a surprise to us when Ell's older sister and her husband contacted us and declared that they wanted to take her two siblings into their home. In a month or so they went to live with their older sister and her husband.

"After all these troubles, in 1870, I had sold half of the mill to Harlin Elliot, and we moved to Logan County where I sold out the other share, my half, to

Harlan Elliot, and then we moved to Hardin County and bought another mill. I sold my land in Logan County, and bought fifty acres there in Hardin County. Then I sold the land and mill and bought fifty-eight acres in Dudley Township, Hardin County. Here, I got into trouble and went into security on some notes, and had to pay it, and that caused me to sell my mill and land. When I went to sell my land, I found a larger mortgage than I had expected, and that caused me to lose $206.86. Well, I paid it all and moved to West Liberty. That is when I had purchased an interest in a marble shop, and this was like jumping out of the frying pan into the fire, for again, I got into trouble.

"Our son, Charles Benjamin, whom we called Ben, was born on April 8, 1871. My parents, wife, daughter, Ella, and I still lived in West Liberty. In 1872, I began to work in the marble trade with my brother-in-law. It was a great learning experience for me. I learned to cut marble, crystal and other fine items.

"It was a shock to me to be sent for at work because my mother had died which darkened the home circle. It seemed to us that the center around which the family circle revolved was gone. O how lonely the home without mother.

"I kept working at the marble shop. I traveled to Columbus in buckboard to pick up marble slabs, or to buy wholesale crystals. I worked with new customers to customize table tops, counter tops, flooring, and other home and business items.

"Our daughter Lizzy Jenetta had been born on March 28, 1875. Soon after that, while working with my brother-in-law for about eight years, I had become dissatisfied with the way he had done business, and with all that I saw as dishonesty in the trade itself. I could not sell a first class job when I knew well that it had actually been from a second class stock in order to compete with other shops; nor could I promise a job to be put up at a certain time, and then not put it up for six months. I couldn't just quit because Lizzy was a baby, Ben was only four, and Ella was ten. Father was not well, so I waited my time and saved money the best I could. When Father died in April of 1877, I earnestly began to seek other employment. In fact, in late 1877, I went to Beloit, Ohio that was near Warren to check on some land, but it didn't appear to be what I had wanted. I just kept looking, and biding my time. I was not happy with my situation. Father had been my oak of honesty and goodness. Memories of his life swept over me for months.

"On May 7, 1880, little Lizzy died from a sickness she took rather sudden. Death just couldn't let us be. It was hard on us all, especially the children this time. Ella and Ben had seen three of their siblings die.

"Two weeks after Lizzy died, we were visited with one of the most destructive fires in the life of the little village. This was about seventeen years after I had come home from the war, and many sorrows had been ours, but knowing Jesus over threw it all, but why did death and disaster follow me?

"When the fire broke out, the whole town was in an excitement such as not common to see: women running fingers through their hair and crying, children were picked up by other adults, business owners tried to salvage goods, and men tried in vain to put out the fire all that afternoon up to midnight. It wasn't until four o'clock in the morning that the fire had become controlled. The next day had mostly been taken up searching for stolen goods such as groceries, clothing, and dry goods of all kinds.

"We had put away quite a lot of paints, oils, and other notions from different firms that we had used in our shop. I reported this to the insurance investigators who had been in our shop. Time passes on, and things go quiet. Insurance policies were paid out, and then building began—this time with bricks. In a rather short time, there were several large buildings in progress, so things, soon after the fire, went on as before. I concluded that I would finally change our business, for it wasn't even as good as it had been. I sold my part to my partner, and sold my house to the cashier at the Logan County Bank. During sale of my shop and the house, I had heard of a place for sale in Morrow County, so I went to see it, for I thought that I could buy a good home now, for I had $1200.00 in the bank and a note of $700.00 from the cashier at the Logan Bank that was to be cashed in a year.

"I bought a place in Morrow County with sixty-four acres from the heirs of Griffith Yevering for $3800.00. I paid $1200.00 on which it left me in debt for

$2600.00. There were wagons, a general stock of tools, and a house to live in, but that cost me more than I had planned. I kept up the table of payments, and paid my debts as fast as I could with the health I had.

"I made an offer for sixty-four acres in Morrow County on December 20th. The trade was with S. Gevering for $3800 at 6% interest for ten years."

The Baldwin Farm

The farm remained in the family until the early 1950s when it was sold by Stephen's son, Charles (Ben) Baldwin.

"I worked the farm for about ten years, but little by little my health began to hold me back. My wife and children saw what had been happening to me. My episodes of shaking and of seeing lights as though visions, were becoming more frequent. My wife had seen that there was something wrong for years, and one time during an episode said to the children, 'Pa is not going anywhere. He will be fine.'

"It seemed that through the years, memories were hard to forget—death of parents, children, fires, and war: the sweat and blood, the fevers, and loss of friends. They all seem unbearable at times. What would I do without my faith?

"In 1881, we had moved to Morrow County, and settled on the farm with the children who helped as they were able, but life was not as I had imagined as a young man. On January 4th, I sold my horse for $100.00. Then on the 5th, I went to town and bought a horse for $95.30. On the 6th, I went back to town and traded a horse with Foust and gave him $5 for the difference. The next day I was able to haul one load of wood.

"I went to Bellefontaine to the sixteenth annual reunion of the 96th Regiment and had a nice time. There were eight soldiers present. This day, 18 years ago, we captured 4,000 rebs. Years ago, after I joined the Grand Old Army group, I did try to go annually."

Stephen' Grand Old Army Ribbon: Front and Back

The GAR (Grand Army of the Republic) was founded on April 6, 1866, on the same principles of a fraternity or charity, by Benjamin F. Stephenson in Decatur, Illinois. Initially, the GAR grew as a *de facto* political arm of the Republican Party, the party of Abraham Lincoln. This all took place during the frenzied political contests during the Reconstruction Era. The GAR promoted voting rights for black veterans.

The Republican Party gradually decreased its reform in the south and the GAR lost some of it momentum. By the 1870s, many divisions or posts had ceased to exist or had little participation. In the 1880s, under new leadership which provided their main platform for new growth, they wanted federal pensions for veterans.

The GAR was organized into "Departments" at the state level and "Posts" at the community level, and interestingly, they wore military-style uniforms. These "Departments" and "Posts" were in every state in the United States and they had several posts overseas.

Membership was strictly limited to "veterans of the late unpleasantness."

In 1868, Commander-in-Chief General John A. Logan is said to have established May 30th as Decoration Day, later called Memorial Day.

DIARY EXCERPTS OF 1881:

"I worked on marble and some other stones, whenever I could, but I busied myself the best I could on the farm: hauling wood in from neighboring farms, and cutting wood off of neighbor's farms, repairing equipment, farming, and sorting out the memorabilia that I had collected from the war. I had Union soldier's caps and uniforms, buttons and chevrons, and other odd things. I put them all in the attic, and over the last ten years, tried not to bother with those things because of memories that came back. Sundays and Wednesdays I went to church."

"In early April, my back was so lame, that I had to stay home a couple of days. This usually occurred when riding my horse. I still managed to sell wood and sugar to make money. I sold twenty-six pounds of sugar that month for twenty cents. That doesn't sound like much but with my pension, preaching, selling headstones, and hauling wood, we had a fair life. I had to borrow sixty

dollars from the bank for only thirty days, May 7th to June 7th. Once in awhile I would fix and set tombstones which paid as much as sixteen dollars. It was fortunate for me when on June 2nd, I received an update in the mail informing me that I would continue to receive my pension."

"I ride over to the Soldiers Home in Dayton at least every three months. What a shock it was when I heard that President Garfield had been shot."

"In July, I had to hire a new hand to help with the farm. I was sick for more than a week. Same thing happened in August, but had to call the doctor. I had to go to Bellefontaine but when I arrived, I was told that my acquaintance, Albert Hogue, had shot and killed a colored man."

"In August, I had to get my buggy repaired. I paid $18.50 with a due balance of $6.50. The next month we went to see Uncle Ransom, and we stayed for the Baldwin Reunion. Then we went to Richard Baldwin's where the next reunion on Thursday, September 3, 1882 would be held. We then went back to Uncle Ransom's place."

"The first of November, I went to see Joseph, my older brother. I became sick for about a week and could not leave the house. This sickness is part of the chronic diarrhea I have had for twenty years."

CALL TO THE MINISTRY

"The years passed, my children got older, my wife was tired, and I turned fifty-five years old in 1891. I had known for a long time that I had a call to the ministry, but I kept it still. Of course, this burden had been a trying and considerable weight on my mind, and the doctrine of sanctification pressed on my mind. I had come under the pungent conviction for the subsequent work of faith. My health began to fail even more, and I was not able to work the farm as I had needed to do. My son Ben was about twenty, and he did most of the work on the farm. I had tried to help but there were days that I could not do much because of the diarrhea and the aches and pains. My wife Ellen was not well and friends sent letters assuring her of their prayers."

Stephen heard his "calling" at the age of fifty-six during a time that his wife, Eleanor (Ellen) was not well. He lost his *"morning star,"* Ellen, who died at the age of 46 on October 24, 1891, approximately twenty-three years after he was discharged from the war and within months of Stephen entering the ministry.

"In the late spring of 1891, I was sitting in an arm chair in the sitting room, and my wife was standing near me. I began to weep bitter tears, so she thought that she could soothe my sorrow again, and she read a short paragraph that was in a newspaper. Then she asked me how I had liked it, but I had been too choked up with tears and could not speak at first. I tried to tell her that I could not think about what she had read, but she was not easily discouraged, so she came over to me and put her loving hands over my face in a soothing way, and in a rather imploring voice said, 'Pa, what is the matter, for I am uneasy about you,' and her tender voice touched the cord so long that had lain still. I said that I had never done anything for Jesus, and as I said those words, the muscles in my arms knotted and my hands drew shut. What a struggle. Something seemed to say to me, 'now *or never: now or never.' I raised my right folded hand toward the heavens, and said, 'Lord, I will.' As quickly as the flashing of lightening, my whole being was permeated with glory. So sudden was the experience that I scarcely knew where I was... My condition was like a volcano whose fiery center was so convulsed that the earthly hill would tremble at times... God had a work for me."*

Stephen's decision to enter the ministry may have been greatly influenced by that fact that his great uncle, John Baldwin helped found the Congregational Church in Atwater, Ohio in 1818. Stephen grew up hearing of his uncle and a strong religious upbringing was his foundation.

Stephen Baldwin in Wisconsin wearing his minister's coat with fellow church members, circa 1895.

Stephen's lineage included that of his second cousin, John Baldwin, who helped found Baldwin Wallace College in Ohio which was considered a religious college. His great uncle, Ransom Baldwin had been a Major in the Civil War, and he had earlier run the Underground Railroad from his farm in Atwater which hid, housed and fed runaway slaves. Ransom was a lay minister when Stephen entered the ministry at which time he gave Stephen his Adam Clark Commentaries, a set of six volumes bound in leather which he had purchased for $5 each in 1833.

Baldwin Reunion circa 1920

Membership ribbon given to original members

Ransom, at the age of eighty-eight, founded the famous Baldwin Reunion on October 14, 1880 in Alliance, Ohio. Stephen's father, Roswell, was a religious man, raising his children to read, memorize scripture, and pray. Stephen was raised in a home that had regular family "alter". These set a-side-times for family devotional gatherings after dinner, followed by school work. His father, Roswell, was a very religious man.

"In about four or five days, a message came that asked me to attend a meeting. I attended, with much anxiety, but soon I was attending many meetings and learned how to preach. By late June, I was a member of the Brethren Church, and soon I had been licensed to preach. I preached in various churches in revivals and special meetings. My wife Eleanor went with me, and was happy that I was doing better. She actually became more involved in my ministry, but she could not always attend, for she was not feeling well, and this brought us both great pains, for she had been ill for some time. We tried our best to stop the ravages of disease through much prayer and two doctors, but it seemed so stubborn to yield, and she gradually went down. I had to be at home with her for about eight months. I watched over her, but the doctors brought no purpose. She was ready for heaven at forty-six years of age, and for immortal glory. On the 24th of October 1891, she bid us farewell just before she had left us. With her eyes closed to the world, my twenty year old son, Ben, laid his hand on her face and asked if she knew who it was, and she faintly whispered, 'If I could see, I would.' As he spoke the name of Ma, she said, 'It is my Bennie.' He could no longer restrain his feelings, and burst into tears of the deepest grief and sorrow, and in a few moments, she was safe in the arms of Jesus. He was her Savior since she had been sixteen. After her internment, we all turned to go to our homes that seemed now more like a home of solitude and loneliness, for we had just buried the light of that home, and again, the way before us appeared dark.

"Added to this trouble was that my dear oldest daughter, Ella, must now leave for her home about one hundred and thirty miles away which added greatly to my pain. My only son, Ben, was all that I had left now, for Ella soon headed back east to her home, and to me, it was as if all was gone. Of course, my son made it as pleasant as he could.

"I had written some poems and hymns while I had cared for my wife during her illness. Here is a short stanza from a hymn about heaven:

There, age will not this body change
Nor sin the soul dismay,
But in a world of glory range
In one eternal day.

"I had been alone many hours reading all these poems and hymns, and thinking about the events in my life, and wondering how Ben was doing with all his chores and carrying his own memories. Rev. Jonah Baldwin had married my son and his bride Jennie on the 25th of December 1889. Sadly for Ben, his wife passed just ten-years after they wed. At the age of twenty-eight, September 20, 1899 after many years of suffering, she left this life probably from some kind of cancer. She had a hole in her side that had required daily tending. Her folks didn't care for Ben or his family. She stayed with her family because often Ben had to follow work. He worked at odd jobs, the farm, and finally the railroad, even becoming an engineer after his second marriage. He loved Jennie so and did the best he could to care for her and their son Walter, who also was ill. Because of Ben's traveling, Walter eventually lived with my daughter, Ella, but Walter passed at her home in 1901, the same year Ben married Elnora Kemerly on May 2, 1901.

"I tried my best to keep up correspondence with officials in the Church, and with ministers I had known, but did little traveling and preaching for a spell until I had collected my thoughts and prayers for guidance as to what I should do."

Stephen received a letter from his daughter Ella stating that he should ride down sometime. He responded by saying he would in about a week. Ella then sent a letter to Ben, asking him to speak with their Pa about the ride down because she had changed her mind due to all of the rain they recently had, and because she didn't want him to ride such a small horse that far. However, Stephen went anyway.

Lodema Baldwin, Stephen's second wife

One day Stephen took a trip back to Atwater, his father's home township in Portage County, and while there he had been reacquainted with a woman that the family had known for some time. Her name was Lodema C. Sherman. He had known Lodema (nee Robb) when she had been married to Edward Sherman, also a Deerfield native. They had known each other since about 1880. This was about the time of Stephen's daughter Lizzy's death.

Baldwin Family Picture circa 1880. Stephen is standing second from right, with his hands on his wife Eleanor (Ellen), with his second wife-to-be, Lodema sitting next to Ellen.

Stephen and Lodema moved to Newark, Ohio, and in 1920, at the age of eighty-four, after many years of ministry, he was simply working in the yard and around the house, and writing letters to friends and family. In a letter to his children he wrote the following on September 15, 1920:

> Dear children,
>
> I got your letters a few days ago. I was not feeling well, nor was grandma. We had too much to see but we joined the Shepherds to take a ride to West Virginia. We started a little after one o'clock in the morning, and we got to cross over the state line about ten before noon. We spent some time until about four, and then we started home through the rain. The road was as good as could be made the most of the way. After we left Flint Ridge... the roads were so crooked, right and left, and up and down, but our machine worked well the whole eight hundred miles, but O' how tired we were...

On April 25, 1922, and still suffering from the Civil War with chronic diarrhea, he wrote to his children:

> Dear Children,
>
> I sit down to write a little letter before I go to roost. I feel pretty fair. The diarrhea is better now, even for two or three weeks, but grandma is not so well, but she is up working with her corns. It is raining tonight.
>
> Well, I put in some onions today after making some screen frames. We put two of them in the windows at the back of the house upstairs. I made a small garden, but it is not much because of the rain... I am writing this with my new pen.
>
> Now grandma has gone to bed.
>
> O' planted some potatoes. I got the lot right next to our lot, and had it plowed, and I mean the lot I had purchased last year, I have planned to rent it out if I can. I think that I will quit farming.
>
> Now I believe that I will go to bed and let this day lay toil for tomorrow.
>
> Good night.
>
> Well this morning is very hazy and dark, but we are up. Too wet to make the garden, so I will do something else. I will go to my big chair that I am fixing to sit in... My paper is out. Goodbye. Write soon or sooner.
>
> Paw S.H.B.

Stephen's daughter-in-law, Jennie and grandson, Walter circa 1888

Stephen's daughter Ella had married and had three children. Ben had married and had a son named Walter. While Ella was Stephen's obedient daughter who shared her father's religious ideals, Ben was the rebellious one and did not get along with his father. After his mother's death, Ben drifted away from Stephen who could not understand why his son would not speak with him. This caused Stephen much heartache and grief.

Charles Benjamin Baldwin circa 1900

On June 6, 1898 Stephen wrote:

"Dear Bennie, my own dear boy. I thought I would write you a few lines tonight. I am quite sore and tired, but that does not bother me like the report that my dear boy is drinking, no I could stand it better to hear you were dead, if you were saved, than to hear you going to a drunkards grave... give your heart to the Lord, and give your Pa some rest.. Jennie came here last Friday, but I have not seen her since... O' I think of my son, and imagine him in a saloon with the drunken mobs, and his sainted mother looking over the battlements of heaven, and looking at the dreaded scene... good-bye Bennie. You won't drink any more will you? Do promise me. Your Pa."

On February 14, 1899, Stephen was in Findlay, Ohio and had received a letter from Ben who needed some money for his family. Stephen wrote:

"Dear son, I am at home again. I got here last night. I was not well at all, for I had diarrhea... I pray God will bless you in your finances, and here is five dollars, and I sent the overcoat today. When I get my pension, I will send some more... Well good bye for now, your parents, S.H. and Dema."

No one quite knew what was going to be Stephen's response when speaking to him or corresponding whether in person, telegram, or letter.

On March 6, 1899 Ben told Jennie in a letter that he had received a letter from his father and that neither of his parents were well.

On June 14, 1899, Jennie said in a letter to Ben, "When I went to town yesterday, your Pa was a little cool, but I don't say anything. I didn't tell him about what you said about drinking." She was leaving for Cardington to be with her family. She told Ben to sell one of the farm machines to help with debt. On March 9, 1899 Jennie had written to Ben that Stephen gave her a half of a pound of cotton and gauze for her open wound in her side. Stephen could be considered "cool" toward some people throughout his later life, but was ever ready to help whenever he had felt the opportunity or urge.

Ben tried to quit drinking according to a letter to Jennie on March 14,

1899. He often asked her and others, in letters, to pray for him because of his past drinking problems. On March 19th, he answered her, *"Well Jennie, you don't have to think you spite me one bit by writing so much..."* She was not well and in a lot of pain, and that was all she had, just writing letters.

Within nine months of this letter she had died. It was difficult for Ben and Jennie, because of the in-laws, his moving around for jobs, and Jennie needing her parents to help in her last months. Stephen and Ellen were not well enough to care for Jennie each day, even if they had wanted to give her help.

Ben was not earning enough to help Stephen and his mother pay for Jennie's doctors and hospital care, and to pay for what he needed on the road. Every time a new job came up, he sent a new address. This was quite trying on him, with little encouragement from his father, Stephen. He tried to go to church often to keep from drinking. His parents and Jennie wanted him to remain free of alcohol, and for most of 1899, he did good, and went to church when he could go.

In one letter he told Jennie he wrote: *"I didn't give a dime to a man who boards with me. He would get a bottle, and I wasn't gonna be part of that."* Ben grew up a responsible working man, in spite of a troubled father. Stephen had planned to move from the farm, and buy a house, and told this to Jennie and Ben in March, so Ben was going to quit his current job the first of April of 1899 and move into the farm house his father had owned to work on the farm and care for Jennie.

On April 16th, Jennie wrote to Ben, *"... and about coming up to move, Pa changed his mind and is not going to move until a week from Saturday... well Pa is in a hurry,"* she said in closing, and she wanted to get the letter in the mail. By this time Jennie had to have someone write some of her letters, and she was still having difficulty eating. Twice she asked Ben in a letter not to get the blues over her. Because of the increasing disability as the disease progressed, she had sores on her back, and the incision on her lower abdomen which required bandage changes quite often.

Ben was doing all that he could to get home to the farm to care for his wife and their son Walter. When he did get home, he did all of the packing and moving of the household from Cardington where Jennie and Walter were staying near her parents. On May 5th he was back at the farm working in Morrow County, but she had to stay in Cardington with family because he could not work and care for his wife and son as he had originally planned.

After Jennie's death on September 20, 1899, Walter, now eight-years-old, was moved into his Aunt Ella's (Ben's sister) household and cared for by her. Out of concern for Walter's care, one of Jennie's sisters wrote a letter to Ben on November 16, 1899. *"I saw dear little Walter and I took him in my arms and kissed him... he will be ruined if he stays there. Don't tell that to anyone. I love your sister Ella, but she has children that tell lies about Walter. I told Ella that wasn't right. They say right in front of him that he is a liar, and the little fellow looked so petrified that it made me mad... sorry, perhaps this is enough."*

Ben was in a constant state of turmoil throughout most of 1898 through 1901. It seemed that his life was a constant struggle with trying to find work, his battle with alcoholism, and his wife Jennie's tragic illness. The most painful struggle for him was due to his son Walter's unknown sickness which ultimately took his life in 1901 at the age of ten, just two years after Jennie had died.

In 1901 Ben Baldwin married his second wife, Elnora Elizabeth Kemerly while estranged from his father, Stephen. Regardless of his father's plea to reunite with him as father and son, the relationship remained broken. His father, the Civil War soldier passed on the 14th of June 1923.

One of the last letters written by Stephen to his prodigal son shows the pain he was enduring over the broken relationship:

"I feel so bad to know you have got so bitter against me for nothing. I suppose I might as well say good bye, sever, and forever. You will think of me when I'm gone. Think over the Quaker's grave yard, then think that I'm not there. Your far broken Father."

On August 19, 1934, at 6:15 am, on the back porch off of the kitchen in the Baldwin farmhouse, with his two grandchildren, his son, and his second wife in the house, Ben sat alone with his last thoughts and a double barreled shotgun. He committed suicide at the age of sixty-three.

POST TRAUMATIC STRESS DISORDER OF STEPHEN HAMLIN BALDWIN

In his own words, prior to the war he was a healthy, strong, young man. While in the Civil War, he sent a letter to his wife that he had been told by a physician that he has suffered a sunstroke, and another told him that he had a "soldier's heart", after which he wrote to his wife that he had heart disease from sunstroke.

He said in his diary that he could not share everything about the war with Ellen, his wife.

Stephen's traumatic war experiences included illness that plagued him from early training in Kentucky. He had seen many dead soldiers from time to time as most soldiers had. He had been surrounded by confederates who were combing the field and searching the brush, as he hid in a thorn bush with only his revolver, when he had been inadvertently left behind, and three days later, in the same area, he saw a dead soldier from his regiment who had washed up on the shore of the Mississippi River after being shot three days before during the battle along the Yazoo River. The bloated, dark body was something again that just added to the death toll. When he reached Arkansas Post on the Mississippi River, it was a large battle that the 96th Regiment had been heavily involved. He describes in detail, the scene during and after the three days of this intensive battle. They took over 3,500 Confederate soldiers prisoner and shipped them all north. Many died on the way.

The last two letters from him during the war described two things: his chronic diarrhea, and thoughts of desertion to Canada. Stephen went from a gung-ho attitude of "go kill slavers" to a sickly young man who had seen men from his regiment die in skirmishes and then in the major battle of Arkansas Post.

He had an inability to remain on an even keel, for his ship had been blown by the winds of war, the loss of children, the burning down of his house, and taking on his wife's siblings when he was hard pressed to financially to care for them. Then there were the emotional breakdowns that progressively had grown worse until his death in 1923. PTSD is often so debilitating that it becomes like a ghost that haunts which cannot be controlled.

At the age of fifty-six, another uncontrollable emotional experience that worried his children, led him to the ministry. His wife could not consol him this time.

He had been raised a Methodist, but chose the evangelical Brethren Church for his ministry. He completed home study courses and some schooling at a ministerial school and had been licensed to preach; however, he never took a church—just filled in around Ohio, Wisconsin, and Pennsylvania and had less stress as a result. His relationships were tedious with family, both wives, and his two surviving children.

He loved his country and his Baldwin heritage. When the attorney Charles Candee Baldwin published the Baldwin Genealogy, from 1500 to 1881 in 1881, he learned of this work in the 1890s and found that he had been from the line of Joseph Baldwin who had arrived in a New England in 1638 on the *Martin*. He had met with a newspaper reporter in Morrow County who had brought this work to his attention.

Stephen loved to read poetry and had written many poems and sermons. These things brought him solace, and a sense of purpose, for he had been so misunderstood because he had been misdiagnosed.

He served his country with sweat and blood, and became another true American who journeyed an uneven course, but found a sense of peace at the end.

REFERENCES

Baldwin, Charles Candy, 1834-1895. Baldwin Genealogy from 1500-1881, The Leader Printing Company, Cleveland, Ohio, 1881.

Baldwin, Stephen Hamlin, 1836-1923. Diaries, hand crafted items, letters written by him and to him, and pictures.

Harper's Weekly, a Journal of Civilization, Vol. Vi.—No.294, New York, Saturday, August 16, 1862.

Hirst, K. Kris. "The Irritable Heart, Increased Risk of Physical and Psychological Effects of Trauma in Civil War Vets" on internet at About.com Education Psychology, Free 2006.

JAMA Network| JAMA Psychiatry| http//archpsych.jamanetwork.com

Silver, Roxane Cohen, PhD, Professor & Director of Graduate Studies, Department of Psychology & Social Behavior, Department of Medicine University of California, Irvine 2006. "Physical and Mental Health Costs of Traumatic War Experiences Among Civil War Veterans" by Judith Pizarro, PhD; Roxane Cohen Silver, PhD, and JoAnn Prause, PhD. (Dr. Silver sent this study to me.)

Ohio Genealogy Express-96th O.V.I. "Roster of the 96th Regiment Ohio Vol. Infantry" www.ohiogenealogyexpress.com/military/96th_OVI_coH.htm

APPENDIX

John Baldwin, 13 October 1799 – 28 December 1884

Co-founder of Baldwin Wallace College

He was born in Branford, New Haven, Connecticut, and moved to Berea, Ohio in 1827. He was a pioneer in the grindstone business which he developed into a large trade. He had been a plain and economic in his personal life, but had been of a large generosity and a great public spirit. He co-founded Baldwin Wallace College. He felt quite interested in the early settlement of Kansas. Baldwin City, Kansas was named after him.

Dwight Hamilton Baldwin September 15, 1821 – August 23, 1899

He was born in Erie County, Pennsylvania, and in 1862 he relocated to

Cincinnati, Ohio, and establishes a piano and organ company. He had been a teacher of the reed organ and violin, with the help of his staff, he creates the Baldwin piano and builds the first vertical piano in 1891. The Baldwin grand piano was introduced in 1895.

Ransom Baldwin July13, 1802 – October 1886

He was the second child born in Atwater, Ohio in a cabin. He was a lay minister, and before the Civil War, and he ran an Underground Railroad through his farm house. In 1861 he joined the Ohio 81st Infantry under Colonel Thomas Morton which joined General Fremont in Missouri. They were called Morton's Independent Rifle Regiment. He had become a Major leading some of the Independent Rifles.

When he came home as a Major, the name stuck, and from then until his death, he was called Major Baldwin.

Stephen Hamlin Baldwin, 4 November, 1836 – 14 June, 1923

He had been a farmer, artisan, veteran, and minister.

He had joined Company H, Ohio 96th Regiment in August 1862 and served until March of 1863. He served as a minister for about twenty-seven years.

LINEAGE ORGANIZATIONS

Sons of the Union Veterans of the Civil War 1861 – 1865
The Sons of Union Veterans of the Civil War is a fraternal organization dedicated to preserving the history and legacy of heroes who fought and worked to save the Union. Organized in 1881 and chartered by Congress in 1954, they are the legal successor to the Grand Army of the Republic. National website: www.SUVCW.org

The Sons of the American Revolution is the leading male lineage society that perpetuates the ideals of the war for independence. As a historical, educational, and patriotic, non-profit corporation we seek to maintain and

expand the meaning of patriotism, respect for our national symbols, the value of American citizenship, and the unifying force of "e pluribus unum" that was created from the people of many nations -- one nation and one people.
National website:
www.NationalSocietySonsOfTheAmericanRevolution.org

The General Society of Mayflower Descendants
www.TheMayflowerSociety.org

The Order of the Founders and Patriots of America
www.FoundersPatriots.org

General Society of the War of 1812
www.SocietyOfTheWarOf1812.org

Jamestowne Society
www.JamesTowne.org

Daughters of the American Revolution (DAR)
The Daughters of the American Revolution is a nonprofit, nonpolitical women's volunteer service organization dedicated to promoting historic preservation, education and patriotism.
National website: www.DAR.org

www.ingramcontent.com/pod-product-compliance
Lightning Source LLC
Chambersburg PA
CBHW060212050426
42446CB00013B/3055